NEVER to be RELEASED

VOLUME 2

More true-crime titles by Paul B. Kidd

Never To Be Released: Australia's Most Vicious Murderers

Australia's Serial Killers: The Definitive History of Serial Multicide in Australia

The Knick-Knack Man: Inside The Mind of Australia's Most Deranged Serial Killer

PAUL B. KIDD

NEVER
to be
RELEASED

VOLUME 2

HarperCollins*Publishers*

HarperCollins*Publishers*

First published in Australia in 1999
by HarperCollins*Publishers* Pty Limited
ABN 36 009 913 517
A member of the HarperCollins*Publishers* (Australia) Pty Limited Group
www.harpercollins.com.au

Copyright © Paul B. Kidd 1999

The right of Paul Kidd to be identified as the moral rights author
of this work has been asserted by him in accordance with
the *Copyright Amendment (Moral Rights) Act 2000* (Cth).

This book is copyright.
Apart from any fair dealing for the purposes of private study, research,
criticism or review, as permitted under the Copyright Act, no part may
be reproduced by any process without written permission.
Inquiries should be addressed to the publishers.

HarperCollins*Publishers*
25 Ryde Road, Pymble, Sydney, NSW 2073, Australia
31 View Road, Glenfield, Auckland 10, New Zealand
77-85 Fulham Palace Road, London W6 8JB, United Kingdom
2 Bloor Street East, 20th floor, Toronto, Ontario M4W 1A8, Canada
10 East 53rd Street, New York NY 10022, USA

National Library of Australia Cataloguing-in-Publication data:

Kidd, Paul B. (Paul Benjamin), 1945- .
  Never to be released 2.
  ISBN 978-0-7322-5981-5.
  1. Violent crimes – Australia. 2. Criminals – Australia.
  3. Murder – Australia – Case studies. I. Title.
364.10994

Cover photo and design by Luke Causby, HarperCollins Design Studio

To Christine and Peter Simpson and their sons, Zac and Tas. It was the murder of their beloved daughter and sister, 9-year-old Ebony, that brought about the formation of the Homicide Victims Support Groups throughout Australia which have since helped so many people like themselves to cope with the heartache of losing a loved one to homicide.

Some good does come from all evil.

Acknowledgements

As always, the Corrective Services Departments of NSW and Queensland have been most helpful and co-operative. Many thanks to Bob Stapleton in NSW and Roger Carstens in Queensland for their kind and courteous service.

Maureen Doughty of John Fairfax Research, for the most courteous, efficient and reliable information service a writer could wish for. An absolute pleasure to do business with.

Luke Morfesse of the Western Australian and Martha Jabour at the NSW Homicide Victims Support Group, Charles Wooley and Steve Barrett of *60 Minutes* and my partner, Jenny Greene, for invaluable assistance with research and editorial input.

And special thanks to my literary agent, Trish Lake, of Freshwater Productions, Sydney, for her tireless efforts in bringing the project together.

About the Author

Paul B. Kidd is a Sydney-based author, photo-journalist, magazine editor, Radio 2UE broadcaster and freelance *60 Minutes* researching producer who specialises in true crime, big-game fishing, humour and adventure.

Paul's articles, interviews and photographs have appeared in most Australian major outdoors and men's publications and in numerous magazines and websites worldwide.

Paul B. Kidd is a recognised authority on Australian serial killers and criminals who have been sentenced to life imprisonment, never to be released. He is the author of ten books and lives in Sydney's Eastern Suburbs with his partner, Jenny.

Contents

INTRODUCTION
1

Chapter 1
The Arguments for and against Capital Punishment
25

Chapter 2
The Threads that Link Australia's Serial Killers
39

Chapter 3
'Keep My Daughter's Killer Behind Bars'
John Lewthwaite
58

Chapter 4
Mr Stinky
Raymond Edmunds
68

Chapter 5
The Griffith Schoolboy Murders
Michael George Laurance
73

Chapter 6
The Russell Street Bomber
Stanley Brian Taylor
85

Chapter 7
The Japanese Tourist Murder Mystery
Robert Raymond Day
90

Chapter 8
The Lonely Hearts Killer
Rodney Francis Cameron
95

Chapter 9
Ebony: the Murder of Ebony Simpson
Andrew Peter Garforth
103

Chapter 10
The Geraldton Axe Murderer
William Patrick Mitchell
114

Chapter 11
The Central Coast Massacre
Malcolm George Baker
117

Chapter 12
The Murder of the Little Girl on the Pink Bike
Robert Arthur Selby Lowe
120

Chapter 13
The Backpacker Murders
Ivan Robert Marko Milat
140

Chapter 14
The Bodies in the Shopping Bags
Edwin Street
152

Chapter 15
The Port Arthur Massacre
Martin Bryant
155

Chapter 16
The Mysterious Death of Jodie Larcombe
Daryl Francis Suckling
159

Contents

Chapter 17
Murder in the Outback
Brendan and Vester Fernando
165

Chapter 18
The Bow and Arrow Butcher
Richard William Leonard
174

Chapter 19
The Crime That Touched Australia's Heart
Paul Wade Streeton
184

Chapter 20
Natural Born Lifer
Earl Heatley
190

Chapter 21
The End of 'Mr Smack'
Wing Piew Chung
193

Chapter 22
The World's Worst Hit Man
Gary Zane Glasby
196

Contents

Chapter 23
The St Valentine's Day Murderer
Lindsey Robert Rose
201

Chapter 24
Australia's Most Notorious Gangster
Arthur Stanley 'Neddy' Smith
206

Introduction

This is a book about the most horrendous crimes imaginable. These atrocities were all committed in Australia, not in America or England where horror seems to be almost an everyday event, and the likes of beasts such as the Moors murderers Myra Hindley and Ian Brady, serial killers Fred West and Ted Bundy and cannibals such as Jeffrey Dahmer are household names.

We have our own collection of monsters. And as we don't hang them any more, much to the disgust of the majority of the population, who would love to see them strung up or put down by lethal injection, we lock them away, never to be released.

What you will read in this book defies comprehension. And before you start reading it, think hard about whether or not you can handle the shocking events that are ahead of you — I haven't pulled any punches.

But then again, I haven't embellished any situation just for the sake of sensationalising it either. What you will read is exactly what happened.

Unlike authors who probe into the heads of these beasts and visit them in prison, I have never met any of the monsters you will read about.

Introduction

I don't want to meet them. I don't want to look across a prison table at a fellow human being – and I use the term loosely – who has committed unspeakable atrocities and try and figure out what made him (or her) do it.

Writing about true crimes is testing enough; I certainly don't want to meet any of these real-life child killers, mass murderers and serial killers. As FBI honcho Jack Crawford warned trainee Clarice Starling as she went to interview the psychopathic serial killer Dr Hannibal "the Cannibal" Lecter in *The Silence of the Lambs*: 'Starling, be very careful. Believe me, you don't want Hannibal Lecter inside your head.'

Similarly, I don't want any of the monsters in this book running around in my head. Researching them at a distance is bad enough. Besides, this is not a book about what made them do what they did. This is a book that tells the facts, what happened. Nothing more, nothing less.

This is a book about people who are members of a very exclusive club: they will remain in prison for the rest of their lives, no matter how long that may be. They have been given the harshest punishment the system can dish out – life imprisonment with no fixed non-parole period, or the recommendation that they are 'never to be released'.

A recommendation that a person is 'never to be released' is not made lightly by the authorities, and the proof of that is that almost all the Australian murderers whose files have been so marked are still in prison, and that is probably where they will die.

Until recently, the recommendation that a prisoner be incarcerated without the possibility of parole was

Introduction

reserved only for our most horrific murderers: the mass murderers, those who rape and murder in pairs and packs, the child murderers, the serial killers, the psychopaths who murder complete strangers.

But the list now includes a drug dealer, a man who was found guilty of the attempted murder of a tourist after being acquitted of the murder of another tourist, and a man who threw petrol over a child and set him alight. You will read about these three cases in this book.

Research indicates that the first time it was recommended that a prisoner never be released was in the case of 17-year-old Lionel John Roberts, who shot and killed a grazier in NSW in 1936. The sentence was handed down after his original death sentence by hanging was commuted to life imprisonment. Roberts was eventually released and, ironically, in 1987, at age 69, he murdered Margaret Teresa Parer, 27, in Queensland, and was again sentenced to life in prison.

But history shows that Roberts was a rare exception. Not so fortunate as to be granted the freedom to kill again are schoolgirl murderer Lenny Lawson, whom the NSW Minister for Justice, Mr Mannix, recommended 'never be released' in 1962, and Australia's first modern-day serial killer, William 'the Mutilator' McDonald, who murdered four derelicts in 1963 and had his papers marked 'likely to offend again', indicating that he would never be released.

Both Lawson and McDonald are still in prison almost four decades later, and that is where they will die.

But it was the horrific crimes of Kevin Gary Crump and Allan Baker in 1973 that deep-etched the term 'never to be released' into the Australian

Introduction

vernacular. Fresh out of prison, the pair murdered and robbed farmhand Ian Lamb as he slept in his car. They then abducted Mrs Virginia Morse from a secluded farmhouse at Collarenebri in rural NSW and repeatedly raped and tortured her, then eventually murdered her and dumped her body in a river over the Queensland border. They were finally captured near Newcastle, NSW, after a wild, running gun-battle with police. In passing sentence on the unrepentant pair, Justice Taylor said: 'The description of "men" ill becomes you. You would be more aptly described as animals, and obscene animals at that. I believe that you should spend the rest of your lives in jail and there you should die.'

Then Justice Taylor added the statement that has become the yardstick for numerous 'never to be released' recommendations handed down since:

If in the future some application is made that you be released on the grounds of clemency or of mercy, then I would venture to suggest to those who are entrusted with the task of determining whether you are entitled to it or not, that the measure of your entitlement to either should be the clemency and mercy you extended to this woman when she begged you for her life. You are never to be released.

But as irrevocable as Justice Taylor's words sounded, it was revealed in May 1997 in NSW that in law, judges have no legal ground to order that a prisoner should never be released – that power lies with the government. The term 'never to be released' has caused a legal row, with experts claiming the phrase is meaningless and could be legally challenged.

Introduction

This is all very well in theory, but the vast majority of prisoners who have been sentenced to life with the recommendation that they never be released are still in prison today.

This is evident in the cases of some of Australia's most horrendous murders since 1960:

- Of nine serial killers, one was hanged (Eric Edgar Cooke, the Perth 'Midnight Murderer', in Fremantle Prison in 1964) and the rest are still in prison. With the exception of the 1993 'Frankston Serial Killer', Paul Charles Denyer, who was granted a 30-year non-parole period on appeal, all have had their papers marked 'never to be released' or were sent to prison with no fixed non-parole period.
- All the child killers who have had their papers marked 'never to be released' are still in prison or have committed suicide in prison.
- All those who abducted, raped and murdered in pairs or packs and had their papers marked 'never to be released' are still in prison.

Every State in Australia has its own set of laws, and so the words 'never to be released' mean different things in different places. In Tasmania, for example, if a sentencing judge says a person is never to be released, then those words become the law, and the prisoner is destined to die in jail.

In NSW, the 1989 truth-in-sentencing legislation now ensures that a life sentence means life and the prisoner will never be released. Adding the term 'never to be released' is the judge's prerogative.

Introduction

In SA and Victoria, if a prisoner is sentenced to life without a fixed non-parole period, that means he or she is never to be released.

According to the Western Australian Law Society, a law was passed in 1996 in WA, stating that if a prisoner is sentenced to life imprisonment with the judge's personal recommendation that he or she never be released, then that is the law, and the prisoner will stay in jail forever. Western Australian judges also have the power to deny a prisoner the right to ever make an application for a non-parole period to be set. The case of William Patrick Mitchell, the Geraldton Axe Murderer, is the only example of this thus far.

Queensland judges started handing down the 'never to be released' recommendation in 1990, when child murderers Barrie John Watts and Barry Gordon Hadlow, career criminal and dual-murderer Francis James Carter and attempted murderer Robert Raymond Day were all sentenced to die in jail. Since 1990 there has only been one other prisoner in Queensland who has received the same recommendation: Paul Wade Streeton (in 1996) for throwing petrol over a boy in a schoolyard in Cairns and setting the lad on fire. Queensland is second only to NSW in the number of 'never to be released' recommendations handed down.

In the Australian Capital Territory (ACT), a life sentence doesn't mean exactly that, and a prisoner is permitted to apply to have a non-parole period fixed. According to the ACT Law Society, no prisoner has ever been sent to jail there with the recommendation that he or she never be released.

Introduction

The maximum sentence in the Northern Territory (NT) is mandatory life, but a prisoner can apply to have a non-parole period fixed. A spokesperson for the NT Law Society could not recall the term 'never to be released' ever having been used in the Northern Territory.

In *Never To Be Released*, published in 1993, I wrote of thirteen cases in Australia from 1961 to 1990 where the murderers had received this recommendation from either a sentencing judge, court-appointed psychiatrists or the Minister for Justice. The cases are:

William McDonald, now 74, (the Mutilator), mild-mannered homosexual mail-sorter, for the serial murders and removal of the sexual organs of four derelicts in Sydney in 1961–62. McDonald, Australia's first modern day serial killer, is in maximum security in Cessnock Correctional Centre, and has been behind bars for 36 years. After more than three decades behind bars, McDonald is 'institutionalised'. He will die in jail, as his papers are marked 'likely to offend again'. McDonald has never sought release and, according to authorities, he is perfectly happy where he is, living a reclusive existence, reading books and listening to classical music.

Leonard Keith Lawson, 71, illustrator and brilliant portrait artist, for the rape and murder of a young woman and the fatal shooting of a schoolgirl in NSW in 1961. Lawson is in maximum security in Grafton prison and, since he had his application for sentence re-determination rejected in 1994, has resigned himself to the fact that he will die behind bars.

Introduction

Archibald Beattie McCafferty, 48, unemployed alcoholic drug addict, for the murders of three male strangers in 1973 after McCafferty's dead son told him from the grave to 'kill seven...kill seven...kill seven'. McCafferty was one of the most troublesome prisoners ever to be held within the NSW prison system, and was found guilty of the manslaughter of a prisoner in Parramatta prison in 1981 and given a further 14 years. McCafferty only mellowed in the last years of his sentence in the minimum security Berrima prison. On 1 May 1997, McCafferty was taken from prison and deported to his native Scotland, much to the disgust of Scottish authorities.

But even all those years in prison and his new home in Scotland couldn't keep Archie out of trouble. In October 1998, he was placed on two years' probation for threatening to kill police officers near Edinburgh, following a drinking session and argument with his de facto wife, mother of his 4-month-old son.

In Edinburgh Sheriff's Court, McCafferty pleaded guilty to careless driving, driving with no licence or insurance, failing to provide a breath specimen and breach of the peace (after three police cars pursued him at high speed).

Allan Baker, 50, and **Kevin Gary Crump**, 48, ex-convicts, for the cold-blooded murder of farmhand Ian James Lamb, and conspiracy to abduct, rape and murder Virginia Morse in NSW in 1973. Gary Crump is in maximum security in Lithgow Correctional Centre and Allan Baker is in maximum security in Grafton Correctional Centre. Baker and Crump have both appealed for a re-determination of their sentences.

Introduction

Both of Baker's two applications were rejected but, amid massive public protest, Crump was granted the right to seek sentence re-determination in 2003.

James Miller, **59**, the Truro Murderer, ex-convict, burglar and homosexual transient, for his part in assisting Christopher Worrell to abduct, rape and murder six young women in South Australia in 1978–79. Worrell was killed in a car accident before the discovery of any of the missing girls' bodies. Miller is in SA's Yatala prison. He is not considered a security risk.

David and Catherine Birnie, **both 47**, labourer and housewife (the Moorhouse Street Murderers), for the abduction, rape and murder of four young women in Perth in 1986. Catherine Birnie is in maximum security in Bandyup prison and David Birnie is in maximum security Casuarina prison. Both are eligible to apply for parole in 2007.

John Raymond Travers, **31**, **Michael James Murdoch**, **30**, **Michael Patrick Murphy**, **44**, and **Gary Stephen Murphy**, **40**, unemployed criminals, for the abduction, rape and murder of nursing sister Anita Cobby in Sydney in 1986. Another member of the gang, Leslie Murphy, was granted a re-trial in 1990, at which he was again found guilty of the murder of Anita Cobby. In re-sentencing Murphy to life, Justice Badgery-Parker did not include the term 'never to be released', which had been recommended by Justice Maxwell when he first sentenced the five men to life imprisonment in June 1987.

Introduction

Barrie John Watts, 46, armed robber and transient, for the abduction, rape and murder of 12-year-old schoolgirl Sian Kingi at Noosa, Queensland, in 1987. His wife, Valmae Faye Beck, 56, who helped him procure the girl, was also convicted of the murder and sentenced to life imprisonment, but without the 'never to be released' recommendation.

Darren Osborne, 33, the serial rapist who raped and murdered a young woman at Albany, WA, in 1987. Osborne was found hanged in his cell at Casuarina prison in August 1997.

Francis James Carter, 43, long-time criminal, for stabbing a prisoner to death in jail in 1990 while serving a life sentence for bashing a man to death with a baseball bat and then removing his fingers with a bolt-cutter. In recommending that Carter never be released, the judge described him as 'the most dangerous man in Australia'. Carter is in the high security section of Queensland's Sir David Longhand Correctional Centre.

Stephen Wayne Jamieson, 32, **Bronson Matthew Blessington**, 24, and **Matthew James Elliott** 26, street kids with long criminal records, for the abduction and horrific rape and murder of Janine Balding in NSW in 1988. At the time of the murder Blessington was 14 and Elliott 16. They were the youngest offenders ever to have their papers marked 'never to be released'.

John Wayne Glover, 65 (the Granny Killer), respectable rate-paying travelling pie salesman with a hatred for old women, for the serial bashing murders of

Introduction

six little old ladies in 1989–90 in and around the streets and suburbs surrounding Mosman on Sydney's lower north shore where Glover lived with his wife and two daughters.

Barry Gordon Hadlow, 56 (the Carbon Copy Killer), for the abduction, sexual assault and murder of 9-year-old Stacey-Ann Tracey at Roma, Queensland, in 1990. Hadlow had served 23 years in prison for the murder of a 5-year-old girl in Townsville in 1962, and was released in 1985. Hadlow is in the medium security section of the Woodford Correctional Centre.

With the exceptions of Archibald Beattie McCafferty, who was deported, and Darren Osborne, who was found hanged in prison, all the murderers listed above are alive (at the time of writing) and behind bars. And none of them looks like getting out in the immediate future.

There are another 22 prisoners in Australian jails who, according to law, have forfeited their right to ever be free again. All their cases are in this book. They are:

John David Lewthwaite, 43, a psychopathic homosexual paedophile, for the stabbing murder of 5-year-old Nicole Hanns at Sydney in June 1974, while on parole for arson. Nicole was stabbed 17 times, the knife going right through her body three or four times, inflicting injuries to her heart, lungs and liver. The little girl had interrupted Lewthwaite as he was about to abduct her 9-year-old brother and rape him. In sentencing Lewthwaite to life imprisonment, Justice Slattery said he had the utmost concern as to whether Lewthwaite should ever be released, but this was a

Introduction

matter for the authorities. Mr Slattery said, 'Regrettably, there is no future for you in society, and unless medical science can come up with a solution, there appears to be no solution to your psychiatric problems. The ferocity and extent of the particularly savage killing of the child indicate that you are not capable of ever leading a normal life in the community.' Lewthwaite had his sentence re-determined in 1994, and he was deemed eligible to apply for parole, but each time he has applied, he has been rejected.

Stanley Brian Taylor, 60 (the Russell Street Bomber), for his part in the 1986 car bombing in which a police constable, Angela Taylor, was killed outside the Russell Street police station in Melbourne. Life with no fixed non-parole period.

Raymond Edmunds, 54 (Mr Stinky), Victorian dairy farmer, given two life sentences with no non-parole period for the 1966 shooting and bashing murders of two teenagers. Edmunds was also sentenced to 30 years (with a minimum of 16 years and eight months) for three rapes and two attempted rapes and 10 years for sex offences against a 4-year-old girl.

Rodney Francis Cameron, 46 (the Lonely Hearts Killer), for the murder of Maria Goeliner at Katoomba, NSW, in June 1990, three months after he was released from prison for the 1974 murders of a man and woman. Cameron had been jailed 'for the term of his natural life', but was released in March 1990, after serving 16 years in NSW and Victorian prisons. Cameron has since confessed to five other unsolved murders.

Introduction

Robert Raymond Day, 45, labourer, was acquitted in 1990 of the 1988 Queensland murder of Japanese backpacker Noriyuki Oda when police couldn't produce Oda's body. It was eventually discovered in 1993. Later in 1990, Day was tried for an almost identical crime, the attempted murder of a Danish backpacker, and found guilty.

Andrew Peter Garforth, 35, unemployed labourer, for the abduction, sexual assault and murder of 9-year-old Ebony Simpson at Bargo in rural NSW in August 1992. After assaulting the little girl, Garforth threw her in a dam and walked away from her pleas for help. Ebony's parents, Peter and Christine Simpson, helped form the Homicide Victims' Support Group, which now helps people like themselves throughout Australia.

Malcolm George Baker, 51, unemployed, for the shotgun murders of six people on the NSW Central Coast in October 1992. In what became known as the Central Coast Massacre, Baker murdered his son and five others, including a pregnant woman.

Edwin Street, 44, invalid pensioner, for the murders of his wife, who was found buried in a shopping bag in a Sydney park in 1993, and another woman whom he was then living with, who was found in a suitcase in his house two months later.

William Patrick Mitchell, 29, farmhand, for the murder of Karen MacKenzie and her three children at a house 400 km north of Perth, WA, in 1993. Mitchell pleaded guilty to four counts of murder, three of

Introduction

indecently interfering with a corpse and one of sexual penetration of a girl aged seven. Mitchell became the first person under the new WA law to be jailed with no chance of parole.

Robert Arthur Selby Lowe, 61, husband, father, Sunday school teacher and church elder, for the premeditated abduction, sexual assault, murder and concealment of the body of 6-year-old Sheree Beasley in Victoria in June 1991. Life with no fixed minimum term, which is the Victorian equivalent of 'never to be released'.

Ivan Robert Marko Milat, 53 (the Backpacker Killer), road-worker and gun fanatic, for the murders of seven young backpackers between 1989 and 1992. Milat concealed his victims in the Belanglo State Forest, south of Sydney. It is thought that Milat did not act alone in the murders and that he may be involved in other NSW murders.

Brendan, 23, and **Vester Fernando**, 24, unemployed alcoholic and drug-addicted cousins who abducted, raped and murdered nurse Sandra Hoare at Walgett, NSW, on 9 December 1994.

Earl Heatley, 51, long-time criminal, for the murder of two men, one his own brother, during a bungled robbery in Sydney in 1994. Heatley had served 15 years in jail for another murder in 1966.

Richard William Leonard, 25 (Baby Face), boat-builder and abattoir worker, for the bow and arrow

Introduction

murder and dismemberment of Stephen Dempsey in Sydney in August 1994 and the stabbing murder of a Sydney taxi driver in November 1994. Leonard kept Dempsey's body parts in his freezer and used to roll the head across the floor when bored.

Darryl Francis Suckling, 62, property caretaker and sex offender with over 100 convictions dating back to when he was 11 years old, for the 1987 abduction, rape and murder of 21-year-old prostitute Jodie Larcombe at an unknown place in NSW.

Martin Bryant, 31, the Port Arthur gunman, for the murders of 35 people at Port Arthur in Tasmania on 28 April 1996.

Paul Wade Streeton, 28, unemployed charity worker, for the attempted murder of 6-year-old Tjandamurra O'Shane by throwing petrol over him and setting him on fire in a Cairns schoolyard in October 1996. It was the first time a 'never to be released' sentence had been handed down for a crime other than a homicide.

Wing Piew Chung, 44, Singaporean national and high-ranking member of the Ah Kong, an international drug-smuggling organisation, for supplying 63 kg of high-grade heroin with a street value of almost $150 million in NSW in the early to mid 1990s. He was sentenced to life in April 1998 under the NSW Drugs Misuse and Trafficking Act.

Gary Zane Glasby, 41, ex-convict with an extensive record (including violence and armed robbery with

Introduction

wounding), for the 1994 contract killing of John Theissi at Georges Hall in NSW. It is thought that Glasby and his wife, Suzette, were contracted for between $30,000 and $50,000 to make the hit. Glasby was sentenced to life imprisonment, which, under truth-in-sentencing legislation, automatically means 'never to be released'. Suzette was sentenced to 12 years for her part in the killing.

Lindsey Robert Rose, 43, former paramedic and Granville Train Smash hero, also professional contract killer, for the murders of four women and one man in Sydney between 1984 and 1994.

Arthur Stanley 'Neddy' Smith, 53, Australia's most notorious gangster, underworld enforcer, gunman, rapist, heroin dealer, armed robber, murderer and informer, for the 1983 murder of brothel-keeper and drug dealer Harvey Jones. Smith was convicted of the murder of Jones in September 1998, and sentenced to life imprisonment. He was already serving life for the 1987 murder of a tow-truck driver and 13 years for an attempted armed hold-up.

It could be said that the case of John David Lewthwaite, who murdered 5-year-old Nicole Hanns in 1974, shouldn't be a chapter in this book, because Lewthwaite has had his sentence re-determined, with the result that he was given permission to apply for parole 20 years after his original sentencing in 1974. This makes him technically ineligible for the 'never to be released' category.

At Lewthwaite's sentence re-determination hearing in 1992, Justice Slattery said 'there still exists the

Introduction

possibility that he (Lewthwaite) could be a risk to the community, especially young boys'. This was the same Justice Slattery who said in his sentencing of Lewthwaite at his original trial in 1974 that he had 'the utmost concern as to whether Lewthwaite should ever be released' and added, 'you are not capable of ever leading a normal life in the community'.

The judge's recommendations fell just short of the words 'never to be released'. I believe that John Lewthwaite is an outstanding candidate for this book because he should be behind bars forever. And it would seem that the parole board agrees with me.

While Lewthwaite became eligible to apply for parole in 1994, he is still behind bars – his 1994 application and four more annual parole applications have all been rejected.

It is obvious from the above list, and when one considers the length of time that some prisoners have been in jail, that being sentenced to life imprisonment with the recommendation that the prisoner is 'never to be released' is not taken lightly in Australia.

Apart from the aforementioned Lionel Roberts in 1936, prisoners who have beaten the 'never to be released' recommendation are rare. Of the seven examples I could find, three had had their sentences re-determined, one was released and, for the other three, the only way out was death.

Sentences Re-determined

Keith David Herring, now 52, cockney gangster, was convicted in Sydney on 3 October 1991 of the drowning murder of his wife and sentenced to life

Introduction

without parole under the NSW truth-in-sentencing legislation. In September 1994 the conviction was quashed and a re-trial ordered. In December 1985, Herring was convicted of murder and given a minimum sentence of 18 years.

Paul Charles Denyer, 26 (the Frankston Serial Killer), confessed to murdering three young women in Victoria's Frankston district in 1993 and was sentenced to three terms of life imprisonment with no fixed non-parole period. In 1994, Denyer appealed against the severity of his sentence and, much to the disbelief of the victims' families, was granted a 30-year non-parole period.

Willi Twala, 37, a black South African teacher, was convicted in 1993 of the stabbing murder of his wife, Donna Burns, in Sydney, and sentenced never to be released. In November 1994, Twala successfully appealed and was given a re-determined sentence – a minimum 15 and a maximum 20 years.

Set Free

Shirley Ann Conlon, as a 22-year-old, murdered her rent collector in 1978 in barbaric circumstances and as a result was sent to jail for life by Justice Slattery, who added that Conlon 'should hold no expectation of ever being released'. Justice Slattery also sentenced Conlon to an additional 20 years for armed robbery with wounding.

In April 1992, the same Justice Slattery reduced Conlon's life sentence to a minimum sentence of 15 years jail. She was released in 1993. Justice Slattery

Introduction

played an important part in the release of Shirley Ann Conlon, as he conducted an extensive examination of the woman's deprived upbringing prior to presiding over her application to have her life sentence reduced to a determined minimum.

Died

Maxwell Harold Trotter, **44**, was convicted of the sexual assault and murder of a young boy on a farm in rural NSW. Trotter died of natural causes in Long Bay Prison in 1994.

Committed Suicide in Prison

Michael George Laurance, **46**, a homosexual paedophile who murdered three schoolboys at Griffith in rural NSW between September 1984 and June 1986, was found hanged in his cell at Lithgow prison in April 1996.

Robert Mark Steele, **27**, was convicted of murder and being an accessory to the murders of two men in rural NSW in March 1993. Steele and two other men also kidnapped two children and were involved in a 26-hour siege with police near Grafton. Steele committed suicide at Goulburn Jail in December 1994.

Homicide Victims' Support Groups

On a personal note, I must mention that it used to disturb me that the families and friends of the victims involved in the cases I have written about may have

Introduction

thought that I was capitalising on their misfortunes in writing about the tragic deaths of their loved ones and the apprehension of their killers.

As it has turned out, nothing could have been further from the truth. Shortly after the release of my first book on this subject in 1993, I was invited by Martha Jabour, Executive Director of the then newly-formed Homicide Victims' Support Group, to be guest speaker at their monthly meeting.

The group's members consisted of people who had been brought together through the murder of a loved one and the group was formed with the intention of supporting others in their grief over losing someone close to them in a violent manner.

I was surprised at the invitation. In my ignorance, I thought that the last thing the grieving families of murder victims would want would be more death. I assumed that they would want to try to forget rather than be constantly reminded of it. I thought that they would rather sweep it under the carpet, so to speak, and try and put it out of their minds. But I was soon to find out that my assumptions couldn't have been more wrong.

When I arrived at the meeting I was introduced to Grace and Gary Lynch, who thanked me for the story I had written in the book under the title of *The Slaying Of An Angel*, about the horrific murder of their beloved daughter Anita Cobby.

They told me that they were extremely grateful that I had helped keep Anita's memory alive and that the book would play a part in keeping Anita's murderers in jail for the rest of their lives.

Halfway through speaking on the subjects I had chosen for the night, being some of the cases in the

Introduction

book and the arguments for and against capital punishment, I stopped and told the audience of about sixty or so people that I was confused about why they would invite someone along to talk about what I would think they were trying to forget.

In unison they told me that forgetting what had happened to their loved ones was the last thing they wanted to do. They wanted to be constantly reminded of them. They wanted their memories kept alive, never allowed to fade away. And they wanted justice meted out to the people who murdered them.

No. The last thing they wanted to do was to forget.

That night I volunteered for the position of Media Director for the group, a position I held for a few months, until the HVSG got the publicity they desperately needed, so that other homicide victims would know where to go for help, and so that they could get some government funding. I am proud to have played that part for them, as small as it was, but I must confess that it was one of the hardest few months I have ever spent in my life.

At every monthly meeting there would be brave new faces in the crowd, desperately sad to have to be there but ever so grateful to have the shoulders of experience to cry on and someone to embrace who had been through what they were going through now.

Since those early days, more than 600 families have passed through the NSW HVSG and, as a direct result, support groups have started in almost every other State of Australia.

In the chapter in this book entitled *Ebony: The Murder of Ebony Simpson*, you will read about how the murder of Ebony Simpson at Bargo, NSW, in 1992

Introduction

inspired her parents Christine and Peter to form the group.

Thanks to the tireless efforts of foundation members such as Christine and Peter Simpson, Martha Jabour, John Merrick and Grace and Gary Lynch, the HVSG is now a powerful organisation, fighting for the rights of the victims left behind by murder and working constantly to keep the perpetrators of these crimes behind bars.

Capital Punishment

Considering that I have written about almost every horrific murder in Australia in modern times (since 1960) and been privy to the atrocities of those crimes that were never published in newspapers, I have often been asked about my thoughts on capital punishment. Despite having written many thousands of words on the subject, I have never given a public opinion. Until now.

Yes, I believe that in certain cases the killers should be executed. But having said that, I don't believe that the re-introduction of the death penalty would be a deterrent.

And while I'm not going to run out and actively campaign for the re-introduction of the death penalty, to my mind the likes of child murderers such as Barry Gordon Hadlow, Robert Arthur Selby Lowe, Andrew Peter Garforth, Michael George Laurance, John Lewthwaite, Valmae Faye Beck and Barry John Watts shouldn't be wasting the taxpayers' money in prison; they should have been executed long ago, when their appeals ran out.

Introduction

If Barry Hadlow had been executed when he murdered his first little girl, in 1962, then the little girl he murdered in 1990 would most probably still be alive today.

At least Michael Laurance hanged himself in prison.

To my mind, those who rape and murder in packs, such as the killers of Anita Cobby and Janine Balding, should have been put to death a long time ago. With the exception of William McDonald, whom I believe was insane at the time of his crimes, I wouldn't shed a single tear if every killer in the country who was in jail 'never to be released' were put to death.

I believe that the death penalty should automatically apply to serial killers, child murderers and those who rape and murder in pairs or packs.

And that puts the vast majority of the killers in my books in that category.

Paul B. Kidd
Sydney, August 1998

Chapter 1

THE ARGUMENTS FOR AND AGAINST CAPITAL PUNISHMENT:

Should our worst offenders be put to death?

Two weeks after the horrific abduction, rape and murder of nursing sister Anita Cobby by five men in NSW in 1986, a Sydney TV station conducted a phone-in survey on capital punishment. Of the 16,000 callers, more than 95 per cent agreed with the re-introduction of the death penalty

In May 1994, in the NSW Parliament, Tony Windsor, Independent MP for Tamworth, an advocate of capital punishment since the murder of Ebony Simpson, lodged a petition of 400,000 signatures requesting a referendum on the re-introduction of the death penalty 'in extreme cases of murder where there is absolutely no doubt that the offender committed the crime.'

The cold-blooded murder of little Ebony Simpson was one such crime. In August 1992, at Bargo in the NSW southern highlands, Peter Raymond Garforth sexually assaulted 9-year-old schoolgirl Ebony Simpson and then threw her in a dam and left her to drown.

Capital Punishment

Garforth took police to the girl's body and pleaded guilty to the murder.

In sentencing Garforth to life imprisonment with the recommendation that he never be released, Justice Newman said: 'The callous indifference to the fate of his victim by the prisoner would appal any civilised human being.'

It would seem that society agrees that beasts such as Garforth and Anita Cobby's killers are among the lowest of the low.

But while support for capital punishment may ride high when horrific crimes such as the Anita Cobby and Ebony Simpson murders occur, taking another human being's life, particularly when it is done by the state, is a giant step to take, and there are those who equally strongly oppose it.

The last person to be hanged in Australia was Ronald Ryan, in 1967. Ryan died at the end of a rope, but he was a choirboy compared with some of the criminals who are residing in our jails at the moment.

Ryan was a thief and a bank robber who shot and killed a prison warder while escaping from Pentridge jail in 1965.

While there had always been some doubt as to whether Ryan was the one who actually pulled the trigger, he confessed to the governor of Pentridge, only minutes before he went to the gallows, that it was he (Ryan) who had fired the fatal shot and that the law had judged correctly. His confession certainly put a lot of minds at ease.

Just two months after the hanging of Ronald Ryan, Sir Henry Bolte's government was returned with a landslide 44-seat majority. It would seem that the

Worst Offenders Put to Death?

hanging of Ryan had little effect on the people's choice of government.

Although the crime that brought about Ryan's demise was dastardly, it pales in comparison to the ghastly deeds of some of the villains in other States where the death penalty didn't apply.

Had the death penalty not been abolished in NSW in 1955, there seems to be little doubt that Lenny Lawson, the multiple rapist and schoolgirl murderer, would not have escaped the noose.

Leonard Keith Lawson was sentenced to death in Sydney in 1954 for the rape of two young models. He had tied them up at gunpoint and violated them in front of three of their workmates, whom he had also tied up. The sentencing judge, Justice Clancy, was so incensed with Lawson's crime that as the prisoner was being taken away, the elderly judge summoned him back and said:

Before you leave, I want to add this. It is not my practice, where a sentence is fixed by Parliament, to make any observations. In your case I propose to depart from that practice.

I should not want you to leave this court in the belief that you can expect any clemency in any recommendation by me. I accept the law as it is, and I think that it is a proper law, and a just law. I think that in your case there is no reason why it should not be carried out into execution.

(As quoted in Never to be Released, Volume 1)

But the judge's words went unheeded. Amid public outrage, Lenny Lawson beat the death penalty and had his sentence commuted to 14 years in prison.

Capital Punishment

In jail, Lenny saw the error in his ways and gave himself over to God, saying that he found great strength in embracing the Catholic faith. He painted scenes from the Bible on the walls of the Goulburn prison chapel, and clergy came from all over the country to marvel at the work of the reformed man of God.

Thanks to the Lord's help, Lawson was out of jail in May 1961, after having served less than half his allotted time. Six months after he was released, Lawson raped, bashed and stabbed to death a 16-year-old girl on Sydney's North Shore and shot and killed a 15-year-old schoolgirl the following day. Had the Government required the services of a hangman then, there would have been a queue of volunteers a mile long only too happy to pull the lever and watch Lawson swing.

Lenny Lawson has been in prison for 37 years now, and will die there.

Another candidate for the gallows, had they still been in operation, was William 'the Mutilator' McDonald, who specialised in murdering derelicts in public places in Sydney in the pre-Ronald Ryan early '60s.

After McDonald had repeatedly stabbed his victims to death, he removed their genitalia and took his grisly souvenirs home in a plastic bag.

The Mutilator killed four homeless men before the law caught up with him. The judge who sentenced him suggested that the authorities throw away the key.

McDonald and Lawson were both found to be sane at their trials and both were sentenced to life imprisonment with the recommendation that they never be released from prison, where they are to this day.

Worst Offenders Put to Death?

The Western Australian serial killer, Eric Edgar Cooke, was not so fortunate. 'Cookie' shot and killed three men and raped and murdered three women in their homes over a five-year period in Perth in the early '60s.

Cooke was known as 'the Midnight Murderer', as he would break into homes and commit his awful deeds in the dead of night. Cooke died on the gallows at Fremantle Prison in 1964, becoming the last person executed in WA and the second last to be hanged in Australia. A lone protester held vigil outside the prison as Cookie dropped through the trapdoor.

Queensland abolished capital punishment in 1922 and Victoria in 1976. But with the re-introduction of the death penalty in the USA, there appears to be growing public opinion in Australia that we should follow suit and dispose of our most dreadful murderers in a similar fashion.

After Anita Cobby's murder in 1986, almost 20,000 people signed a petition demanding the return of capital punishment.

But while public opinion may be riding high about permanently ridding society of its most dastardly outcasts, there is also a fierce – and not unreasonable – argument that death, being an irreversible punishment, cannot be redressed in the event of a miscarriage of justice, and therefore should not be legalised.

Until recently, the classic cases quoted by the anti-death penalty lobby are those of Timothy William Evans and Derek Bentley. The dim-witted Evans went to the gallows in England in 1950 for the murder of his baby daughter, Geraldine.

Three years later, Timothy Evans' landlord, John Christie, confessed to murdering six women and having sex with their corpses. Their bodies were found in his house. Christie also confessed to murdering Timothy Evans' wife, Beryl, and the baby Geraldine.

John Reginald Halliday Christie went to the gallows at Pentonville Prison in July 1953. The unfortunate Evans was eventually granted a posthumous Royal pardon in 1966. His body was exhumed from Pentonville Prison and reburied in consecrated ground. Legal experts agree that no jury of the '90s could possibly convict Timmy Evans on the evidence offered at his trial.

Although the slightly retarded Evans confessed to the crimes, modern forensic and DNA evidence would have pointed the finger at Christie, the main prosecution witness in the Evans trial, and perhaps saved the lives of four women.

The case of Derek Bentley is the classic misuse of the death penalty and one of the most shameful acts in the history of British justice. Although Bentley didn't pull the trigger and, for that matter, never even held the gun, he was convicted of the murder of a policeman when his associate, 16-year-old Chris Craig, deliberately shot and killed a constable while caught on a rooftop after attempting to rob a store in London in 1953.

The sacrificial lamb, Bentley, was heard to say 'Let him have it', seconds before Craig opened fire.

The prosecution maintained that Bentley was calling to his partner, telling him to shoot to kill. The defence argued that he was telling Craig to hand the gun over and surrender.

The jury chose to believe the prosecution, and because the under-age Craig couldn't pay the ultimate

Worst Offenders Put to Death?

price for the life of the policeman, the epileptic Bentley, a man with the mental age of an 11-year-old, was sent to the gallows, despite mammoth protest from an outraged public.

Criminologists now claim this case is a good example of the classic argument against capital punishment. Chris Craig served 10 years of his life sentence and was released from prison in 1963. He has never come to the attention of police again.

While such travesties of justice did occur in the '50s, experts believe that they would not happen today. Yet, as long as the death penalty still exists, there is always the possibility that an innocent person could be the victim of a miscarriage of justice. When the death penalty is abolished, that possibility does not exist. This, in itself, is a very strong argument against capital punishment.

But while the British justice system has always been the yardstick used in the argument against execution in Australia, the Australian anti-capital punishment lobby now has its own classic case against the re-introduction of capital punishment.

In November 1973, Johann Ernst Siegfried (Ziggy) Pohl was convicted of strangling his wife, Joyce Kum Yee Pohl, at Queanbeyan, in southwestern NSW. He was sentenced to life in prison. He appealed against the conviction but the appeal was dismissed in August 1974. Ziggy stayed in jail.

Ziggy Pohl vehemently proclaimed his innocence, saying that his English was very poor and he did not know that the answers he was giving to the police would be misinterpreted and used against him. But the circumstantial case against him was strong.

Capital Punishment

On the surface, Ziggy was the only person likely to kill his wife. Furthermore, he could not account for his actions at the time of the murder. It looked like an open and shut case.

The only thing missing was the motive. No one could come up with a logical explanation for why the outwardly happy and secure Ziggy Pohl would want to kill the woman he so obviously loved, with whom he shared his every moment.

But, that aside, the kindly German immigrant with the big smile and the sad eyes was bundled off to Long Bay Correctional Centre to serve out his term, amongst the most vile killers in captivity.

Ziggy Pohl was a model prisoner and was released on parole after serving only 10 years of his life sentence. The parole board considered that Ziggy had paid his debt to society and, motive or not, they couldn't see him killing any more of his wives in the future.

Having taught himself to read and write English during his prison years, Ziggy Pohl set about trying to prove his innocence. But his efforts were to no avail. No one would listen and no one cared. It seemed Ziggy would spend the rest of his life with the stigma of being a convicted murderer.

In September 1990, 17 years after Ziggy Pohl's conviction and seven years after his release from prison, the most amazing thing happened. Roger Graham Bawden (aka Roger Graham) walked into the Queanbeyan police station and confessed to the murder of Mrs Pohl. It had been on his conscience for almost two decades and he had to get it off his chest.

When interviewed by detectives, Bawden gave information that only the killer could have known.

Worst Offenders Put to Death?

There was no doubt that he was the murderer and that Ziggy Pohl had been wrongly convicted.

When asked why he had not come forward earlier, Bawden maintained that he had left the district shortly after Mrs Pohl surprised him burgling the house and he strangled her, and had no idea that her innocent husband had been found guilty of his (Bawden's) crime.

Bawden claimed he first heard of Ziggy Pohl's conviction when he returned to his home town, only weeks before he confessed to the killing. He claimed that he had gone all those years thinking that the murder was unsolved.

Ziggy Pohl was unconditionally pardoned in May 1992 and eventually awarded $1 million compensation for his decade behind bars. In a strange irony, Roger Graham Bawden pleaded guilty to murder and was sentenced to only eight years in prison.

But what if capital punishment had been the law at the time of the death of Mrs Pohl? What if Ziggy Pohl had been put to death for strangling his wife? And if capital punishment had still been in force 17 years down the track, would Roger Graham Bawden also have been hanged, for the same murder?

Admittedly, all these questions are totally hypothetical, but they do lay a very solid foundation for the argument against the death penalty.

The fact that Ziggy Pohl was released after serving only 10 years of his life sentence is, in itself, indicative of what the parole board thought of his conviction. In other words, it would appear that there was always some doubt in a lot of people's minds about whether or not Mr Pohl did indeed murder his wife. There was no eyewitness, no confession and no motive.

Capital Punishment

And if he did commit murder, then it certainly wasn't premeditated. It was more of a crime of passion or a violent act committed in a fit of rage. Even the strongest advocate of capital punishment would find it hard to hang a man under those circumstances.

Some of the best legal brains in the country agree that there is no way that Ziggy Pohl would have been put to death even if capital punishment had been in force at the time of the murder of his wife. The late Irwin Ormsby, principal of Teakle, Ormsby and Associates, the firm of solicitors that handled the Ziggy Pohl compensation case, said, 'I believe in the death penalty for murder involving exaggerated violence. But also there would have to be strict guidelines. In my opinion, the Pohl case would never have attracted the death penalty if it was applicable.'

So Australia has its classic case against capital punishment. But while those opposed to the death penalty claim their arguments are strong and well-founded, the supporters of capital punishment can also show very good cause why the perpetrators of shocking crimes should be put to death.

And the supporters of capital punishment appear to be in unison in saying that each crime must be judged on its merits and only those that fall into the 'worst case' category would incur the ultimate punishment.

These crimes are the most evil of the evil – child rape and murder, gang rape and murder, serial killings, mass murder and violent sex murders.

In the eyes of the pro-capital punishment lobby, it is difficult to understand why people who commit these inhuman crimes, and who are judged sane, should be allowed to live.

Worst Offenders Put to Death?

After all, why should they be allowed to take life so cruelly and not pay for it with their own?

They ask: What purpose does it serve to keep them alive? Rehabilitation? Hardly. They say that Lenny Lawson, *Barry Gordon Hadlow and *Rodney Francis Cameron are criminals who should have been put to death in the first place, thus saving four, possibly six, innocent lives. Instead, they were released to kill another day.

*Barry Gordon Hadlow, 'the Carbon Copy Killer', was sentenced to life imprisonment for the sexual assault and murder of a 5-year-old girl in Townsville in 1962. At his trial, a psychiatric report read to the court said, in part: 'There is no treatment for Hadlow's condition and further aggressive sexual offences will occur if he is not kept in a place of safety.'

Neither time, nor God, could cure Hadlow's murderous obsession with little girls. A model prisoner and devout Christian, he was released in 1985 and in 1990 at Roma in Queensland he sexually assaulted and murdered a 9-year-old girl in circumstances almost identical to those of the first murder.

In sentencing Hadlow to jail without the possibility of parole, Justice Shepherdson was scathing in his remarks about how the child-killer was allowed back into society to kill again:

It is quite apparent that a dreadful mistake was made in releasing you from prison in 1985. Your case is a salutary reminder for those members of the community who believe that convicted persons should not be kept in custody.

From what I read in the press and see and hear of discussions on the radio and on the TV, some members of our

Capital Punishment

> community seem to think that instead of sentencing convicted persons to prison, a better course is to require them to attend some sort of therapy course – perhaps sending them to a specified term of listening to poetry.
>
> It seems fairly obvious that you must have led prison authorities to believe that you were safe to be released. But I suspect that probably one of your weaknesses is small girls, and despite having given the impression you were a model prisoner, it would be fair to say that as small girls are not in prison, any weakness you had was not going to be exposed.
>
> I cannot understand how anyone who had the opportunity of seeing the psychiatric report following the Townsville murder could ever have allowed you to be released in 1985.

Hadlow will never be released from prison to molest and kill little girls again, but that is of little consolation to the loved ones of his tiny victims.

*Rodney Francis Cameron, 'the Lonely Hearts Killer', served just 16 years in NSW and Victorian prisons after being jailed 'for the term of his natural life' for the 1974 murders of a man and a woman.

In 1990, just three months after he had been released on parole, Cameron murdered a 44-year-old woman he had met through a matchmaking show on radio 3AW in Melbourne a month earlier. The circumstances of the woman's death were almost identical to those of his previous two victims.

Cameron has since confessed to another 1974 murder, two unsolved murders in Victoria in 1990, another in SA and another in NSW.

This time, Cameron will stay in prison until he dies.

Worst Offenders Put to Death?

While the judge never actually said 'never to be released' in these two cases, one can only wonder whether if he had, they would have been released to kill again.

Pro-death penalty lobbyists would gladly tell you that putting them to death in the first place would most certainly have eliminated any possibility of their offending again. They would also tell you that God has got a lot to answer for in getting these men back on the streets as, in the cases of Lawson and Hadlow, they became devout Christians as part of their 'healing' process.

Understandably, amongst the most vocal supporters of the death penalty are some of the families of the victims. After three teenagers had been found guilty of the abduction, rape and horrific murder of her daughter Janine in Sydney in 1988, and sentenced to life with the recommendation that they never be released, Beverly Balding told a *Sydney Morning Herald* reporter, 'I'd like to see them die. I heard a comment from America recently – 'to try 'em and fry 'em' – and that's how I feel. I have no wish for revenge. People say that bringing back the death penalty is stooping to the level of the criminals. It's not. Stooping to their level would be to terrorise them as they did Janine.'

Other supporters of the death penalty couldn't agree more. It's impossible for them to find compassion for the likes of child-murderers Barrie Watts and his wife, Valmae Faye Beck, and serial killers David Birnie and his common-law wife, Catherine.

Beck and Watts abducted 12-year-old Sian Kingi at Noosa, Queensland, in 1987. Beck watched as Watts tortured and raped Sian repeatedly. Watts eventually stabbed the young girl to death. During the orgy of horror, the only compassion that Valmae Beck showed was to cover her dog's eyes with her hands so that the animal couldn't witness the obscenities happening in front of it.

David and Catherine Birnie abducted, tortured, raped and murdered four young women over a one-month period in Perth, WA, in 1986. Both took part in the killings.

Both trials incited angry crowd scenes in front of the court as hundreds of citizens gathered outside carrying placards supporting the re-introduction of the death penalty.

Detective Superintendent Mike Hagan, the policeman in charge of the Task Force which brought the infamous Granny Killer, John Wayne Glover, to justice in 1990, after Glover had bashed and murdered six elderly women in a reign of terror in and around the harbourside Sydney suburb of Mosman, offered this general opinion on capital punishment in 1993: 'I think that in some cases there is a position for capital punishment. Particularly in horrific and sadistic murders that are "stranger" killings, where the victim is completely innocent of the circumstances, and the facts of death leave no doubt as to the perpetrator.'

You be the judge.

Chapter 2

THE THREADS THAT LINK AUSTRALIA'S SERIAL KILLERS

The term 'never to be released' is synonymous with Australia's modern-day (since 1960) serial killers. With the exception of Eric Edgar 'Cookie' Cooke, the Midnight Murderer, who murdered six people in Perth between 1959 and 1963 and was hanged in Fremantle jail in 1964, all the others are still alive and still in jail.

An analysis of our serial killers' crimes indicates that it is hard to imagine any of them ever being released – the suggestion would cause public outrage.

It is widely believed among criminologists that it was the search for notoriety that brought about the term 'serial killer' in the first place. It was first used in relation to the motiveless killings of two teenagers in a car near Vallejo, California, in 1968.

The killer, calling himself Zodiac, taunted police and the press with cryptic notes, daring them to catch him by giving them clues as to when the next episode of the 'serial' killings would happen. Zodiac also rang talk-back radio shows and told details of the murders that only the killer would know.

Threads that link serial killers

The original Clint Eastwood *Dirty Harry* movie was based loosely on the Zodiac killings but, unlike the film, the real-life Zodiac was never caught. As late as 1974, it was thought that as many as 37 murders could have been carried out by this one serial killer.

Australia's Serial Killers Since 1960

- **Eric Edgar Cooke**, 'the Midnight Murderer'. Mild-mannered truck driver and father of seven who murdered three men and three women between 1959 and 1963 in Perth (WA). Cooke was hanged in Fremantle Prison in 1964.

- **William McDonald**, 'the Mutilator'. Reclusive homosexual letter-sorter who murdered four Sydney (NSW) derelicts in frenzied knife attacks and removed their genitals in what became known as the Mutilator Murders between 1960 and 1962. He was found, after his trial, to be insane. McDonald is still in prison.

- **James Miller** and **Christopher Worrell**, 'the Mass Murderers of Truro'. Unemployed ex-convicts. The much younger and bisexual Worrell raped and murdered seven young women and the homosexual Miller helped him bury their bodies at Truro (SA) in late 1976 and early 1977. Worrell was killed in a car accident before the bodies were discovered.

- **David** and **Catherine Birnie**, 'the Moorhouse Street Murderers'. Labourer and housewife.

Threads that link serial killers

Common-law married couple who tortured, raped and murdered three women and a teenage girl in Perth (WA) in 1986.

- **Michael George Laurance**, 'the Griffith Schoolboy Killer'. Unemployed homosexual paederast labourer who sexually assaulted and murdered three boys at Griffith (NSW) between 1984 and 1986.

- **John Wayne Glover**, 'the Granny Killer'. Respectable travelling pie salesman who kicked, bludgeoned and strangled to death six elderly women in and around the Sydney suburb of Mosman during 1989 and 1990. Glover lived in the area with his wife and two daughters.

- **Rodney Francis Cameron**, 'the Lonely Hearts Killer'. Convicted killer who murdered a woman at Katoomba in 1990 shortly after being released from prison for the murders of a man and a woman in 1974.

- **Paul Charles Denyer**, 'the Frankston Serial Killer'. Unemployed 21-year-old who stabbed and slashed three young women to death in the Frankston district (Victoria) in June/July 1993. One of his victims had given birth only 12 days earlier.

- **Ivan Robert Marko Milat**, 'the Backpacker Serial Killer' or 'the Beast of Belanglo'. Gun-crazy roadworker who murdered seven backpackers and concealed their bodies in the Belanglo State Forest south of Sydney (NSW) between 1989 and 1992.

Threads that link serial killers

Milat was sentenced to seven terms of life imprisonment and had his papers marked 'never to be released' on 27 July 1996.

Is there a common denominator among Australia's serial killers? Were they all mad? No. Only one Australian serial killer, William McDonald, was found to be insane.

Was sex their reason for committing serial murder? Yes, in some cases, but not in all. Was it robbery, revenge or notoriety? No. All of these factors play a part, but none of them is common to every case of serial murder in this country.

Well, is there a link? And if so, what is it?

Yes, there are many. Australia's modern day serial killers have a lot in common.

- They all originally came from working-class or poor backgrounds.
- All of them blundered through their mass murders and could have been caught in the act at any time.
- They all enjoyed killing other human beings.
- None had prepared alibis for when they murdered.
- Every one of them had an overwhelming desire to be caught, whether they knew it or not.
- And every one of them brought about his or her own undoing.

Silence of the Lambs stuff this is not. There is no Hannibal Lecter, Zodiac, Buffalo Bill or Tooth Fairy among this vile lot. There were no cunningly conceived plans. By and large, they murdered random strangers who happened to be in the wrong place at the wrong time.

Threads that link serial killers

Although the motives for 32-year-old Eric Edgar Cooke's rampage of murder, rape and woundings in Perth in the early 1960s will never be known, Cooke left himself wide open to be caught, and when captured, also confessed to two murders he had committed years earlier.

Short in stature, with a flattened face and an extremely obvious harelip, 'Cookie' was not a good looker. But his wife and seven young children loved him, and he was popular at the Perth fruit markets, where he worked as a truck driver. No one had the faintest idea that he was moonlighting as a burglar while the city slept.

Something inside Eric Cooke's head snapped one night in January 1963 — he shot dead three strangers and wounded two others with a stolen rifle in the small hours of the morning. Two weeks later he raped and murdered a 24-year-old social worker and dumped her body on the lawn of her neighbour's house.

At first police weren't sure if it was the work of the same killer, whom they had now dubbed the 'Midnight Murderer', but when, six months later, an 18-year-old babysitter was shot dead as she watched TV, and the bullet from her head matched those taken from the previous victim, they knew that they were looking for the one killer.

Their break came a week later when bushwalkers found a .22 rifle beneath a bush in an inner Perth suburb. Bullets from the gun matched those found in the murder victims, and police put a 24-hour guard on the bush.

Two weeks later the killer returned for the murder weapon. When apprehended, Cooke enthusiastically confessed to all the killings plus two more murders, committed in 1949 (this was never proved) and 1959.

The only explanation that Cooke gave the police for his ghastly crimes was that he 'wanted to hurt people'. There is little doubt that if he had been more cautious about where he left the gun, the killings would have continued, and police still wouldn't have had a clue who they were looking for.

Did Cooke (consciously or unconsciously) leave the gun under the tree knowing that he was running the risk of being caught? It would appear so. There were a million other places he could have left it where it would never have been found.

He certainly didn't hold back when he was arrested and gladly described his evil deeds. He was glad it was over and revelled in the publicity. Had he hoped the gun would be discovered?

We shall never know. Eric Edgar Cooke dropped through the gallows trapdoor at Fremantle Prison on 26 October 1964.

It would also appear that it was an overwhelming subconscious desire to get caught and talk about his killings that brought about the capture of homosexual serial killer William 'the Mutilator' McDonald, who frantically stabbed to death and hacked off the testicles and penises of three derelicts in public places in Sydney in the early '60s.

After the first three bodies turned up with up to 30 stab wounds in the neck and the genitalia missing, McDonald quit his job as a PMG mail-sorter and purchased a small mixed business under the name of Alan Edward Brennan (the name McDonald worked under at the PMG).

Threads that link serial killers

In June 1962, McDonald lured derelict and convicted thief James Hackett back to his new address, where he stabbed him and mutilated his body.

The following morning he dragged the body beneath the building and packed his bags for Brisbane. There he dyed his hair black and assumed the name Alan McDonald.

Two weeks later, after neighbours complained of a vile smell coming from the shop, police broke in. They found a decomposing body beneath the building and assumed it was Brennan, and thought he had accidentally electrocuted himself.

A death notice for Alan Edward Brennan was placed in the paper and his old PMG workmates attended the service. So six months later, when one of his astonished workmates bumped into and spoke with the 'dead' Brennan in the street near where he used to work, he informed the police, who exhumed the body and identified it by its fingerprints as James Hackett.

When an autopsy discovered familiar mutilations on Hackett's corpse, the police at last knew that they were onto the elusive Mutilator. He was tracked down with the help of the newly introduced identikit drawings, which were displayed on the front page of the papers under the headline 'The Case of the Walking Corpse'.

McDonald confessed to the murders and was clearly pleased that it was all over. He was found to be sane at his trial and was sentenced to four life terms, with his papers marked 'likely to re-offend'. Months later, after he attacked another prisoner in Long Bay jail with a slops bucket, he was declared insane. He has been in prison ever since.

Threads that link serial killers

Had he stayed away, he could literally have got away with murder. What made him come back to Sydney, knowing that another man had been buried in his name and that at any minute he could be caught? And why would he frequent the area where he was most likely to be recognised? Was it a subconscious desire to be caught and, like Eric Cooke, tell of his crimes? It certainly seems possible.

The WA husband and wife serial killers, David and Catherine Birnie, also had a burning desire to get caught. They had abducted a teenage girl, beaten her and tied her to a bed at their home, where David Birnie had repeatedly raped her while his common law wife watched. The girl had overheard them plan to kill her that night, but the woman had come into the bedroom and loosened her ropes and she had escaped.

When police questioned the couple, they denied the allegations and said that the girl was a willing party to sex and that she had smoked joints and got drunk with them. It was her word against theirs, and police had no reason to suspect them of any other crimes.

During a long interrogation, one of the detectives said, half-jokingly, to David Birnie, 'Alright, where are the others?', referring to the disappearances of several women in the Perth district in recent weeks.

To the detective's astonishment, Birnie replied, 'There's four of them. I'll take you to them.'

When told of his confession, Catherine Birnie breathed a sigh of relief that it was all over. The two of them led police to a pine plantation outside Perth, where they pointed out the graves of four females, whose ages ranged from 15 to 31, all of whom they had abducted, tortured, raped and either strangled, stabbed or bludgeoned to death.

At David Birnie's instigation, Catherine had strangled one of them in front of him.

So why did Catherine Burnie let the last girl go? To get caught? And why did David Birnie tell the police of the four missing girls when he didn't have to? He could have confessed to abducting the teenager and raping her and been out of prison in a few years. Was it because he wanted it to be all over so that he could get the recognition that he deserved for his crimes? It would appear so.

The mass murders of Truro (SA) are similar. In a 51-day period from Christmas 1976, seven young women went missing.

Two years later, the remains of one of the women was found in a remote paddock at Truro in the Adelaide hills, and a year later another three bodies were found nearby.

Police put up a $30,000 reward and a woman came forward and said that in February 1977, at a funeral, James Miller, then 38, had told her that the person whose funeral they were attending – Christopher Worrell – had murdered seven girls and that he (Miller) had helped him bury their bodies in the Truro district.

It wasn't until the bodies turned up that she remembered the conversation. She had doubted the story was true, as Miller was openly homosexual, and being party to raping and murdering young girls seemed highly unlikely.

But Christopher Worrell was a different story. In his early twenties, Worrell had a history of attacks on women, and had been in prison for an extremely

Threads that link serial killers

violent rape when he met Miller, who was doing time for burglary. They had a brief affair, after which the besotted Miller would do anything Worrell commanded.

Outside prison they teamed up and Miller drove the car while the handsome Worrell solicited young girls, all complete strangers, at bus stops or as they hitchhiked. Once in the car, Worrell set upon them and raped and murdered them.

The killings stopped only when Worrell and his girlfriend were killed in a car accident. Miller was left badly hurt but alive.

After the accident, Miller became a transient, living in parks and refuges until the police picked him up two and a half years later on the say-so of the woman.

Once again, as we have seen in the other cases of serial murder, that one deliberate fatal mistake, that subconscious desire to be caught, was to bring about another conviction.

With not one shred of evidence to link him to the murders, no witnesses, no motive and no confession, Miller could have denied any knowledge of the conversation and could have walked from the interrogation room and never have been convicted of so much as jaywalking, let alone mass murder.

But Miller volunteered: 'Where do you want me to start? There's three more. I'll show you.' He showed enormous relief that it was all over.

Miller was sentenced to life imprisonment with no fixed non-parole period.

But why did he confess? His conscience? Hardly. In July 1984 Miller stated: 'Chris Worrell was my best friend in the world. If he had lived, maybe seventy would have been killed. And I wouldn't have dobbed him in.' So much for conscience.

Miller revelled in the notoriety and has constantly been in the public eye over the years. He wrote a book, *Don't Call Me Killer*, has gone on hunger strikes at Yatala prison and has claimed many times that he is innocent of actual murder.

It would appear that mass murder gave Miller what he so desperately craved – a place in society. Never mind how evil the price had been.

Michael George Laurance, unemployed labourer, murdered three boys aged 8, 11 and 12 between 1984 and 1986 in Griffith (NSW). When caught, he described in intricate detail to stunned police how he held two of his victims in the bath 'until there were no more bubbles', because it gave him a thrill.

Laurance openly solicited his third victim in a public place where the risk of being identified, which is what in fact happened, was enormous. Yet again, was it the subconscious urge to be caught that made him make such a disastrous mistake?

When questioned about the third murder, Laurance told police: 'The other little boys. I killed them too.'

He didn't have to confess, as there was no possible way the police could have linked him to the first two murders. The boys' bodies hadn't been found until a year after they disappeared and there was no way of telling if they had been murdered, let alone sexually assaulted. But like all the serial killers before him, Laurance had to boast about what he had done.

He admitted that he was glad it was over and didn't hold back in telling police of the indescribable sexual

Threads that link serial killers

and mental torture that the boys were subjected to before he finally killed them.

Again, the common thread. The unknown victims, the fatal mistake and the boasting of the other homicides.

Laurance told horrified police that the first two boys were forced to play games, naked, in front of each other and that he repeatedly sexually abused them. When he had done with them, he drowned them in the bath.

With his last victim, the 8-year-old, Laurance sexually abused the boy before filling his mouth with cotton wool and taping over his nose and mouth. Then he watched as the lad suffocated. Laurance was sentenced to prison for life with the recommendation that he 'never be released'.

In November 1995, Michael George Laurance was found hanged in his cell at Lithgow prison.

Rodney Francis Cameron, dubbed 'the Lonely Hearts Killer' because he solicited his last victim from a matchmaking program on the radio, was another serial killer who desperately wanted to be caught and get it all off his chest.

In 1974, 19-year-old Cameron was sentenced to prison 'for the term of his natural life' for the murders of a 49-year-old woman who was found dead with a towel stuffed in her mouth and a 19-year-old man who was found with a shirt stuffed down his throat. This would become his 'calling card'.

At the Sky Rider Motor Inn at Katoomba, three months after he was released in March 1990, Cameron murdered a 44-year-old woman he had met through a matchmaking show on radio 3AW in Melbourne a month earlier.

Threads that link serial killers

The woman's body was found on her back, choked to death. A handkerchief was stuffed in her mouth and secured with a pair of pantyhose wrapped around her neck and a bunch of yellow carnations was lying on her body.

It was like tracking an elephant in the snow. Cameron was quickly arrested, sentenced to life in prison with no possibility of parole and has since confessed to another 1974 murder, two unsolved murders in Victoria in 1990, another in SA and another in NSW.

Of all of the Australian serial killers, there is no stronger example of the common threads than in the case of pie salesman John Wayne Glover, 'the Granny Killer'. Glover was the copybook serial killer, leaving his trademark on each victim. He will go down in history as being in the same league as Jack the Ripper, the Boston Strangler, Son of Sam and the Yorkshire Ripper.

Almost from the beginning of his rampage of horror, Glover, a happily married ratepayer in the Sydney harbourside suburb of Mosman, father of two daughters, was screaming out to be caught.

During the period from January 1989 to January 1990, Glover kicked, bashed and strangled to death (with their own pantyhose) five women aged from 81 to 92 in public places throughout Sydney's North Shore.

During the same period, Glover also indecently assaulted, bashed, robbed and attempted to murder another eight elderly women. All police had to go on was a footprint in blood and the description of a portly, grey-haired man in his mid-fifties who was seen near the scene of some of the assaults and murders.

Threads that link serial killers

He would say later that he murdered the women, all complete strangers and selected at random, because they reminded him of his despised mother-in-law, Essie.

Unfortunately for one more woman, the two young constables who went to question a portly grey-haired man in his mid-fifties who had been seen molesting an elderly cancer victim in a nearby private hospital didn't connect that man with the serial killings.

When they arrived at the man's home they were told that he had tried to commit suicide and was in hospital. They were handed a note that was found beside the man's body. It read: 'Gay [Glover's wife], don't try and understand. Essie started it all. Sell up. Piss off. Go forward. Don't look back. No more grannys, grannys.'

Glover's desperate bid to be caught sat on a desk at a suburban police station until its significance finally dawned on someone and it was passed on to the Task Force detectives. They knew immediately that the jolly pie salesman was their man, but they couldn't prove it. Glover was tailed day and night and on 19 March 1990, he called at the home of a lady friend near Mosman.

When he hadn't come out eight hours later, police broke in. They found the body of a 60-year-old woman. She had been bashed to death and strangled with her pantyhose.

Glover was in the bathtub, barely alive after washing a bottle of sleeping pills down with a bottle of Scotch and making a half-hearted attempt to slash his wrists. When he recovered, Glover was glad it was over and confessed to the six killings in detail.

Threads that link serial killers

Yet again, it was the serial killer who had brought about his own capture.

Paul Charles Denyer was yet another multiple murderer who went about his business of killing with reckless abandon, leaving glaring evidence. When confronted by police, he confessed to his crimes, down to the last grisly detail, without a sign of emotion.

Denyer, a pudgy 21-year-old, nicknamed John Candy after the late funny man, was in fact a cold-blooded killer who stabbed and slashed to death three young women in a seven-week period in Frankston (Victoria) in 1993. None of the victims, aged 17, 18 and 22, was sexually assaulted.

In the eyes of a leading criminal psychologist, Ian Joblin, Denyer was a rare breed of serial killer, murdering his victims at random, without apparent motive. 'He is perhaps the most dangerous criminal this community has ever known. He is able to describe his crimes without a flicker of emotion. He is not legally insane, but [he is] extremely emotionally disturbed,' Joblin told the *Melbourne Age*.

Denyer was always going to be a monster. As a child he slit the throats of his sister's toy bears, and he grew up obsessed with blood and gore movies such as *The Stepfather*, *Fear* and *Halloween*, all of which he watched over and over.

When still a youngster, Denyer slit the throat of the family kitten with his brother's pocket knife and hung the dead animal from a tree branch. He grew into a lonely kid with no friends, obsessed with knives and other weapons. The young Paul Denyer was remembered by his associates as being completely different from other kids. In later interviews, Denyer would admit that he had

Threads that link serial killers

had the urge to kill since he was 14, saying, 'I've always wanted to kill ... waiting for the right time, waiting for that silent alarm to trigger me off.'

In February 1993, the urge to finally kill a human being took over, and he broke into the apartment of a woman he knew, with the intention of murdering her with a knife. Enraged to find her not at home, Denyer disembowelled the woman's cat, spread its entrails through the kitchen and draped the dead animal's body over a photo of a bikini-clad woman on the kitchen floor. He then smeared the words, 'Donna and Robin – You're Dead' in blood across the kitchen walls. He also slashed the throats of three of the cat's kittens and placed them in a bathtub full of water.

On the rainy night of 12 June 1993, Denyer selected 18-year-old Elizabeth Ann-Maree Stevens, as she got off a bus in Frankston. He marched her at knife-point to a park, where he choked her, slashed her throat and dumped her body in thick undergrowth.

On 8 July, in the late afternoon, Denyer attacked 41-year-old Roszsa Toth as she walked home from Seaford station. Ms Toth broke free and hailed a passing motorist as Denyer fled on foot to his car, which was parked nearby. Later that evening he abducted 22-year-old Debbie Ann Fream as she left a local shop. Ms Fream, the mother of a 12-day-old boy, was forced at the point of a fake gun to drive her car to a lonely stretch of road. There she was forced out of the car and strangled with a length of rope Denyer had in his pocket. Denyer dumped Debbie Fream's body in thick scrub and casually drove her car back to Seaford, the scene of his earlier attack on Ms Toth. He parked the car and walked the short distance to his home.

Threads that link serial killers

Denyer returned to Debbie Fream's car the following day and removed the milk, eggs and chocolate that Ms Fream had bought at the milk bar and took them home, along with her purse, which contained her driver's licence and credit cards.

At 2.30 on the wet afternoon of 30 July 1993, Denyer abducted 17-year-old student Natalie Russell as she walked home from college and dragged her into the grounds of the Long Island Country Club, where he strangled and stabbed her to death.

As Denyer was murdering Natalie Russell, two policemen were less than 50 metres away, examining Denyer's unregistered old car after a postman had reported that the driver had been acting suspiciously.

Covered in blood and with the incriminating knife in his pocket, Denyer noticed the police inspecting his car as he walked toward it and quickly turned around and walked home. But he must have known that his time was almost up as his car had been sighted by police at the scene of the other abductions and the attempted abduction. It was as if Denyer was desperate to be caught. A fat young man leaving his car at the scene of the crime every time – it was as if he was wandering around holding up a neon sign saying 'please arrest me'.

And arrest him they did. The following day the trail lead to Denyer's door, but when detectives called no one was at home. They left a card. Late that afternoon Denyer's girlfriend, Sharon Johnson, whom he lived with and who didn't have the faintest idea of his activities, rang the police to say they were home. When police called Denyer was casually sitting on the lounge watching TV and smoking a cigarette. He willingly

Threads that link serial killers

accompanied police to Frankston police station where, after a little prompting, he confessed to the murders in great detail.

Again, there were the glaring clues, suggesting a desperate desire to be caught; the last murder was committed in broad daylight, only metres from where Denyer had left his car. He accepted the police arriving as if he had been expecting them.

Paul Charles Denyer pleaded guilty to attempted abduction and the three murders and was sentenced to prison for the rest of his life, with no possibility of parole. In July 1994, a year after the murders, Denyer's appeal to the Supreme Court against the severity of his sentence was heard. To the astonishment of the loved ones of his victims, he was granted a 30-year non-parole period.

The families of the victims believed that the only possible sentence for Denyer was jail for life, never to be released. It had seemed that no one would argue with that, but the judges of the Supreme Court did. The Director of Public Prosecutions agreed with the families but failed to win High Court approval for an appeal against the reduced sentence.

Only time will tell whether the Frankston Serial Killer will ever be allowed back into society.

The only exception to these threads that sew Australia's serial killers together is the case of Ivan Milat, the Backpacker Murderer, who, along with the deceased Christopher Worrell, shares the dubious honour of being Australia's most prolific serial murderer, with seven killings.

Even against overwhelming circumstantial evidence, Milat pleaded not guilty to the murders that took place

Threads that link serial killers

in the Belanglo state forest between 1989 and 1992. He still maintains his innocence.

Milat is the only Australian serial killer who has pleaded not guilty other than on the grounds of insanity. Informed parties believe that this is because Milat did not act alone, and that there was at least one other person involved in the horrifying killings – the seven young people were used as target practice, sexually molested and tortured before they were ritualistically murdered.

If Milat had pleaded guilty, he would have had some explaining to do and that would have to include whoever he is protecting with his silence.

The tragedy of the killings is that five of them may possibly have never occurred if country police had arrested Milat after English hitchhiker, Paul Onions escaped when Milat tried to abduct him at gun point and fired shots at him on the highway near Belanglo in early 1990.

A terrified Onions reported the incident to Bowral police, who failed to act on the report. In light of Milat's extensive criminal record, a conviction for that offence would no doubt have seen him back in jail for years and thus saved the lives of five young people.

As with all Australia's serial killers, Ivan Milat is 'never to be released'.

Chapter 3

JOHN LEWTHWAITE

'Keep my daughter's killer behind bars'

It was one of the most horrific murders that Australia has ever known. In 1974, 5-year-old Nicole Margaret Hanns was stabbed 17 times, and with such force that some of the blows went right through her tiny body, inflicting injuries to her heart, lungs and liver.

The murderer was 18-year-old John David Lewthwaite, a homosexual paedophile, who, back in 1972, had watched through a window as Nicole's 9-year-old brother, Anthony Hanns, had a bath at his parent's home in Greystanes in Sydney's west.

Lewthwaite fantasised about murdering the boy's parents and abducting, raping and murdering the lad, and two years later returned to the Hanns' house to carry out his evil fantasy.

On his return to the house late on the night of 26 June 1974, Lewthwaite, who was at the time on parole after serving just 15 months of a 6-year sentence for arson, silently cracked a window and removed all the jagged glass, selecting a long sliver to use as a knife on his intended victims.

Discarding the glass and replacing it with a long carving knife from the kitchen, Lewthwaite went to

Keep my daughter's killer behind bars

the little girl's bedroom. He turned on the light, but then realised that he couldn't get the boy outside – he would have to take him through the broken window.

It was then that Nicole woke up. Lewthwaite motioned to her to keep quiet, then rolled Nicole over onto her stomach and murdered her by stabbing her repeatedly in the back and on the arms so violently that when police found the murder weapon in the backyard later, it had been buckled into the shape of a horseshoe.

Lewthwaite later told police, 'I was angry because I missed out on getting the boy, but I felt sick stabbing her so viciously.'

When the girl's screams awoke the family, Lewthwaite fled into the night in his blood-soaked clothing and took a train to North Sydney. He exposed himself to a group of schoolboys there the following day. After going to three churches – he wanted to make a confession but could find no one to confess to – he contacted a parole officer he knew and said: 'I think I have hurt a little girl.' Police were called and he readily confessed to the murder.

In the meantime, police had put Nicole's parents, Peter and Gwen Hanns, through an arduous 10-hour grilling in the belief that they may have murdered their own daughter. Then the lad whom Lewthwaite had broken into the house to rape and murder, 9-year-old Anthony, was also subjected to intense questioning, because of the possibility that he may have been responsible for his sister's murder. When Lewthwaite was arrested later the following day, the Hanns family was released.

At his trial, which was held in December 1994, before Justice Slattery, Lewthwaite pleaded not guilty

John Lewthwaite

to murder but guilty to the manslaughter of Nicole Hanns. Court-appointed psychiatrists agreed that Lewthwaite was sane at the time of the murder and, not surprisingly, a danger to society.

One of the psychiatrists, Dr O R Schmalzbach, said he believed Lewthwaite had an obsessive, compulsive, uncontrollable and irresistible urge to kill young boys. He said that Lewthwaite's homosexual drive was directed particularly towards young boys, and that he also liked to expose himself.

Dr Schmalzbach said that when Lewthwaite saw that the girl had awoken, he saw her as something that might get in the way of his plans, and he killed her on impulse.

Other experts disagreed. They believed that Lewthwaite's behaviour was much more sinister than the killing of a tiny child on an impulse. They believed that Lewthwaite murdered Nicole Hanns because he wanted to kill someone, anyone, and for that reason he would be a danger to society for the rest of his life.

They believed that Lewthwaite fabricated his supposed reason to kill the child. They believed that Lewthwaite killed her because he wanted to, not because he felt he had to. It was a senseless waste of a young life.

It took the jury one-and-a-half hours to find Lewthwaite guilty of murder. In sentencing him to life imprisonment, Justice Slattery said he had the utmost concern as to whether Lewthwaite should ever be released, but this was a matter for parole boards in the future.

After being told that Lewthwaite was already under heavy protection in prison because he had killed a child, Justice Slattery recommended that the utmost possible protection continue and added:

> *Regrettably, there is no future for you in society and unless medical science can come up with a solution, there appears to be no solution to your psychiatric problems. The ferocity and extent of the particularly savage killing of the child indicate you are not capable of ever leading a normal life in the community.*

And as John David Lewthwaite was led away to spend the rest of his life in prison, Nicole Hanns' parents, Gwen and Peter, assumed that the nightmare was over. Their daughter's killer was in jail, apparently never to be released.

But they were very wrong.

In 1975 Lewthwaite escaped from Morisset Psychiatric Hospital. He was recaptured quickly. When he escaped again in 1985 after being allowed out of Long Bay jail on day leave to see his psychiatrist, the Hanns' house was put under 24-hour surveillance, as police feared he would return to kill the boy. He was recaptured two days later.

Lewthwaite's escape and rapid re-capture made public the fact that he had been allowed to leave Long Bay jail, unaccompanied, to visit his psychiatrist in the city, when he had committed one of Australia's most appalling crimes only ten years earlier. Not only the Hanns family was amazed.

Reliving the horrors of that night back in 1974, Gwen Hanns broke down and sobbed when she heard of Lewthwaite's escape and, in an emotional interview, expressed her disgust with the prison system and demanded to know why a child-killer was allowed to wander the streets alone. No answers were forthcoming.

Gwen Hanns said at the time: 'It [Lewthwaite's escape] brought back everything – the agony we have tried to keep at the back of our minds all these years. If the people who let him out had to go through what we have been through, they would be the first to throw away the key.'

In December 1986, Gwen and Peter Hanns were awarded the maximum $20,000 criminal injury compensation for Nicole's death. In awarding the compensation, Justice Slattery said that following the child's death, the couple had led a secluded life, and Mrs Hanns in particular had become depressed. They installed a burglar alarm and brought a Doberman dog for protection.

'The couple had recovered, to a degree, until Lewthwaite's escape,' Justice Slattery said. 'They had undoubtedly suffered great trauma.'

But worse was to come for the Hanns family. In July 1992, John David Lewthwaite's life sentence was reduced to a minimum of 20 years by Justice Slattery in the Supreme Court of NSW, making Lewthwaite, now a devout Christian, eligible for parole from 25 June 1994. He was also reclassified as a C3 level (low risk) prisoner at Cooma jail, making him eligible for day release.

The decision sent a shockwave through the community and yet again brought back the reality of Nicole's death, now almost two decades on, to the Hanns family.

The NSW Liberal Government's Attorney General at the time, John Hannaford, promised that he would

Keep my daughter's killer behind bars

make amendments to the Sentencing Act, giving the Crown the ability to appeal against such decisions.

Other politicians pledged their support. The conservative Independent MP for Tamworth, Tony Windsor, gave his support, saying that Lewthwaite should be kept behind bars. Labor MP Carl Scully pledged his full support to stop Lewthwaite being given parole or day release, and threatened to have State Parliament recalled from its winter recess over the issue.

But the general secretary of the Uniting Church's Board for Social Responsibility, the Rev Harry Herbert, said that politicians should 'avoid convincing people by radio talkback'.

It is very dangerous when issues of sentencing in particular cases become the subject of public debate. There are proper processes in place to deal with sentencing and parole, and we should allow these procedures to work. The last thing we want is for politicians to meddle in the sentencing of prisoners and argue the toss about individual cases in Parliament, because that's what we will come to.

An emotional Gwen Hanns said that Mr Hannaford's intended reforms did not go far enough and that she would accept nothing less than a watertight guarantee that Lewthwaite be kept imprisoned for life.

Hannaford said that he did not believe Lewthwaite's release was in the community interest, but that to veto his parole would leave the system open to political abuse.

And so Gwen Hanns' battle to keep her daughter's killer behind bars forever began.

John Lewthwaite

Gwen Hanns lobbied heavily against Lewthwaite being granted parole. On 29 August 1994, the Offenders Review Board denied his application for parole but allowed him to participate in a monthly day release program from Cooma jail.

With the support of Mr Scully, Gwen Hanns vigorously opposed Lewthwaite's day release, and their cause was heavily backed by Bob Carr, then the Leader of the NSW Labor Opposition.

Scully alleged that psychiatric reports on Lewthwaite suggested that he would kill again and that prison informants had alleged that Lewthwaite had raped an inmate in jail.

On 6 October 1995 and on 19 July 1996 Lewthwaite was again formally refused parole by the Offenders Review Board. Again, Gwen Hanns had actively campaigned against his release.

Gwen Hanns was there again in 1997, campaigning, writing letters, attending parole board and Serious Offenders Review Council hearings, building her case and demanding psychiatric assessments of Lewthwaite in the ongoing battle to keep her daughter's killer behind bars.

'Look, I don't want the public to think I'm out for vengeance,' she stressed in her 1997 campaign. 'My main worry is other kids, other parents' children who may become Lewthwaite's next victims. What I'm saying is I'd rather he got me than someone else's baby.'

'If he's cured, if he has been treated and tested, then let the doctors tell me – and prove to me he is no longer a danger to society. While I do get sick and tired of fighting to keep Lewthwaite in jail, I'm never going to give up.'

Keep my daughter's killer behind bars

'As long as there's breath in me, I'll never stop this fight,' she said.

Gwen Hanns even compiled a list of 22 criminals who were released from jail after serving time for serious crimes but who repaid society with murder.

On 2 May 1997, Gwen Hanns had a resounding victory in her ongoing battle with the system. With Bob Carr's Labor Government now in power in NSW, Lewthwaite's application for day release, which is the first step on the road to parole, was rejected by the Corrective Services Commissioner, Dr Leo Keliher.

Instead, Lewthwaite was transferred from Cooma to Long Bay Correction Centre's new Metropolitan Reception and Remand Centre and placed on an in-jail work program.

In June 1997, Lewthwaite broke his 23-year silence and, in a letter to *The Sydney Morning Herald*, claimed that it was politics, and not the fact that he had cold-bloodedly murdered a child, that was keeping him in prison.

Lewthwaite explained that he wants to be accepted as a man who has come to terms with his homosexuality, has a long-term partner and has overcome the urge to sexually abuse boys, a man who has taken God into his life not simply to improve his chances of parole, but to provide spiritual guidance.

'I am not an evil, cold-blooded killer,' he said in the letter. 'If I knew 23 years ago that the torture of uncertainty I would be put through when I finally was eligible for parole, the light at the end of what seems to be a tunnel that goes on forever and is all but extinguished whenever a politician who knows nothing about me except a 23-year old crime decides

John Lewthwaite

to jump up and down for his votes, if I knew that I would be made to feel like the most despicable person alive by people who generate nothing but hatred, then I would never have applied to be released from jail.'

He went on to say that he feels eternal remorse for his crime but believes he has earned a future out of prison. 'If there had been a death penalty in 1974, I would have gladly placed the noose around my own neck,' he said. 'What's done can't be undone.'

Gwen Hanns wouldn't have a word of it, saying, 'He had over 20 years to say he's sorry – why now? Because he thinks it will get him out.'

Lewthwaite's homosexual partner, Brian Craig, a sex offender who did 3 years in the same cell and fell in love with Lewthwaite in Cooma jail, is leading a group of people who are actively campaigning to get Lewthwaite freed.

'He is a political prisoner and it is all about revenge,' Craig, 61, said. 'Every time he gets close to getting day release, politicians jump up and down and stop him. I don't think there is another person in NSW who knows John as well as I do.'

'There is no way he would ever attack a boy or have sex with a boy. I know him and I know homosexuals. No paedophile would entertain an adult relationship and he has one.'

On 2 March 1998, the Serious Offenders Review Board rejected Lewthwaite's annual application for parole, saying that Mr Lewthwaite should remain in jail because he would not be able to adjust to normal lawful community life, there was a risk that he would re-offend, he needed further participation in a pre-release program and his release would not be in the public interest.

Keep my daughter's killer behind bars

Lewthwaite was given the chance to appear before the board and present his case for release at an open public hearing held on 27 April 1998. At this hearing Lewthwaite presented his case and the board heard arguments against his release from Gwen Hanns and Dr Rod Milton, forensic psychiatrist.

The board reserved their decision and on 22 May 1998, they announced their decision: Lewthwaite would stay in prison and be eligible for another parole application in 1999.

When he does apply, you can bet that Gwen Hanns will still be waiting for him.

Chapter 4

RAYMOND EDMUNDS

Mr Stinky

When police routinely fingerprinted a flasher for indecently exposing himself on 16 March 1985 at Albury (NSW), they had no way of knowing immediately that the man was the serial rapist and dual murderer known as 'Mr Stinky'.

Mr Stinky had been on Australia's 'most wanted' list for almost two decades, but it wasn't until the surprise result came back from the police fingerprint files that detectives were finally able to put a name, Raymond Edmunds, to the violent sex offender and murderer.

The irony of the arrest was that if Edmunds, 41, a Victorian dairy farmer, had exposed himself at nearby Wodonga, in Victoria, where police aren't allowed by law to fingerprint suspects as they are in NSW, he may well have continued to elude arrest for murder and rape, as he had done for the previous 19 years.

The murders and rapes that resulted in the arrest of Edmunds started in the quiet Victorian country town of Shepparton, 220 km north of Melbourne, on 10 February 1966, when two teenagers, Abina Margaret Madill, 16, and Gary Charles Heywood, 18, both of Shepparton, disappeared. They had last been seen driving away from a pop concert at the local Civic Centre.

Mr Stinky

Their bodies were found 16 days later in a paddock 30 km away. Gary Heywood had been shot in the temple with a .22 calibre rifle. Abina Madill's half-naked body was found 250 metres away. She had been raped, then bashed to death with the butt of the rifle. Her stockings were found 50 metres from her body in a bushy cow paddock. Each stocking had been double looped and knotted, as though one had been used to bind her hands and the other to tie her feet.

Police believed the teenagers had been taken on a 'death ride' after being abducted at gunpoint from a local lover's lane where they had gone after leaving the concert. The press dubbed the case the 'Lover's Lane' killings, and Melbourne detectives described the crime as 'one of the most vicious and baffling murders ever'.

Despite an extensive police investigation, in which many Shepparton residents came under suspicion, police never found the murder weapon or charged anyone with the crimes.

But they did manage to lift a couple of faint, unidentified fingerprints from the bonnet of the dead man's car.

These would be the undoing of the couple's killer almost 20 years later.

During the 1970s and the early 1980s, Melbourne's eastern suburbs residents were terrorised by a sometimes-masked, barefoot, sandy-haired, beer-gutted rapist whose victims were usually women at home alone with their children. He often raped his victims, at the point of a butcher's knife, in front of their children.

At first named 'the Donvale rapist', he was re-named Mr Stinky by the press because of the peculiar body odour he emitted as he assaulted his victims.

Raymond Edmunds

It is believed that Mr Stinky was responsible for up to 32 rapes in the area during this period, and all police had to go on was a few fingerprints left at the crime scenes. The prints didn't match anyone on their files.

The first police breakthrough came in June 1982, when an observant fingerprint expert noticed a similarity between the Mr Stinky rape case fingerprints and those taken from Gary Heywood's car in 1966.

On closer scrutiny, the prints matched up perfectly. Now that the police knew that Mr Stinky and the Lover's Lane killer were one and the same person, a task force was set up to track the offender down.

But despite almost two years of intensive police investigation, during which they interviewed and eliminated hundreds of men as suspects, the task force turned up no new leads or evidence. It was eventually disbanded in 1984.

It was in March the following year that Albury police picked up Raymond Edmunds for exposing himself in public. They couldn't believe their luck when, five days later, the man they had thought was a minor offender turned out to be Australia's most wanted rapist and murderer.

The day after the fingerprint identification, Shepparton detectives picked up Edmunds, in the Melbourne suburb of Highett, and charged him with the murders of Abina Madill and Gary Charles Heywood and five sex offences.

As it turned out, police had uncovered a secret monster who, while appearing respectable and hardworking, had raped and beaten his wife, sexually molested his daughters and was reported to have once beaten a cow with a shovel for 15 minutes.

At his committal hearing in October 1985, Edmunds pleaded guilty to the Lover's Lane murders and said that he thought about the murders every day of his life and wished that he had been caught earlier.

Edmunds said that he met Madill and Heywood in Shepparton and he and Heywood had sex with Madill. He said Heywood was jealous, believing Madill had enjoyed sex more with him (Edmunds), and that Heywood produced a .22 rifle and started firing it at things.

Edmunds claimed that Heywood then walked away, and it was then that he (Edmunds) shot him twice. When Madill tried to run away he hit her with the gun, crushing her head.

On 4 April 1986, Edmunds was sentenced to life imprisonment, without a fixed non-parole period, for the murders. On 28 October 1986, Edmunds was sentenced to a further 30 years on three counts of rape and two counts of attempted rape. The offences took place in Melbourne between 1971 and 1977. This sentence was reduced to a minimum term of 16 years and eight months in December 1993.

In August 1994, rejecting Edmunds' application to have a non-parole period fixed for the two murders, Justice Cummins said: 'Given the execution of these two innocent young people in 1966, the nature of the offences, and the rape of Ms Madill, and given the past history of Edmunds, being the three rapes and the two attempted rapes during the 1970s, I am satisfied that the nature of the offence and the past history of the offender make the fixing of a non-parole period inappropriate.'

Raymond Edmunds

In September 1998, Edmunds was sentenced to a further ten years in jail after pleading guilty to sex offences committed between 1972 and 1979 against a girl who had been only four years old when they started.

Mr Stinky is behind bars forever, never to be released.

Chapter 5

MICHAEL GEORGE LAURANCE

The Griffith Schoolboy Murders

If it wasn't for crime, Griffith, the soil-rich Riverina district town of 22,000 residents, situated in the southwest of NSW would be better known for its magnificent oranges and grapes, which attract thousands of itinerant workers to the district each year, moving from one place to the next, mainly through the warmer months, picking the fruit, garlic and onions as they come in season.

But sadly for the hardworking folk of Griffith, their town is better known for its crimes than for its agriculture. It is a reputation that Griffith doesn't deserve.

In Griffith in the '70s, a bankrupted Italian ex-panelbeater turned crime boss and Mafia associate, Robert 'Aussie Bob' Trimbole, emerged as the marijuana king of Australia, and Griffith became known as the marijuana-growing capital of the southern hemisphere.

It seemed there were some pretty big Mediterranean-style houses down that way, and the market gardeners who owned them had a lot of trouble explaining to the authorities where they got the money to build them. They were known locally as 'grass castles'.

Michael George Laurance

Then in July 1977, Griffith was back in the headlines when anti-drug campaigner Donald Mackay went missing, presumed murdered. His body has never been found.

And then, almost ten years later, just as battle-scarred Griffith was shaking off its troubled past, a series of killings, more ghastly than anyone could imagine, and enough to make the town's past almost pale into insignificance, would shock the nation to its very soul and put Griffith in the spotlight yet again.

In June 1986, police charged 36-year-old labourer Michael George Laurance with the murders of three schoolboys at Griffith between September 1984 and June 1986.

Laurance had been arrested thanks to observant locals, and as he confessed his crimes in intricate detail, even hardened detectives were revolted to hear of the horrors that the boys had been subjected to as Laurance sexually molested and eventually murdered them.

Little is known of Michael George Laurance's childhood except that he was born in Sydney and raised in the town of Narrabri in northwest NSW. Court records show that Laurance claimed his father was an alcoholic who deserted his mother when he was very young, and he was brought up by his mother and stepfather.

Laurance claimed that from the age of 11, he swapped sexual favours with older men in the district for alcohol and money.

While he used the older men as a source of income, he soon discovered that he much preferred young boys. He started having sex with them and, still in his teens, started collecting photos of naked boys.

The Griffith Schoolboy Murders

Laurance left school at 14. He worked on local farms and took positions as a labourer.

In 1973 Laurance was convicted of indecent assault against a boy in Narrabri and spent time in a psychiatric hospital in Orange after he tried to commit suicide when the mother of a young boy he had been seeing called a halt to the unhealthy relationship.

Michael Laurance moved moved into the Montana Guest House in Griffith in 1983. The Montana Guest House was a clean and inexpensive rooming house with friendly guests. The tall, unobtrusive, red-haired 33-year-old man with the long side-levers fitted in well with the other country folk, and in time some of the kindly people of Griffith would come to like and trust Michael Laurance, the pederast and sexual sadist who had fantasies about molesting, inflicting pain on and killing little boys and who had had relationships with over 150 pre-pubescent boys since his early teens.

They would admire his supposed keen interest in junior football and swimming; in fact Laurance was eyeing off the young boys in the change rooms and becoming aroused looking at their almost naked bodies through the wire fence around the swimming pool.

Laurance said little about his past except to say that he was a recovering alcoholic who was fond of his late mother and that it was the death of his de facto wife and young son in a head-on car smash that had driven him to drink. This was never confirmed and is highly unlikely to be true.

Laurance's entrée into Griffith's hospitality was at the local AA meeting place, which he attended regularly in his ongoing battle with the bottle. From here he was referred to the Community Youth Support Scheme by the clinic's director. He became close friends with this man, and worked part-time as a cleaner at the clinic while studying to become an ambulance driver.

While they never complained about the quality of his work, from all reports, Laurance gave most of the staff at the CYSS the creeps. His moods would change dramatically and he was very aggressive to the male members of the staff and had trouble taking orders from them.

Most of the people who worked there agreed that there was something odd about Laurance, and that they didn't like the way he hung around the young boys in the workshop.

Laurance quit his casual cleaning job and took up doing odd jobs and collecting furniture for the Smith Family. One of the staff who befriended him was Maureen Singh, an effervescent cooking teacher originally from Yorkshire.

Laurance was particularly fond of her teenage son. He explained away the attraction by telling the family that the boy reminded him of his son, who was killed in the car accident, and that they shared the same name – Andrew.

In an interview with *The Sydney Morning Herald* after Laurance's conviction for triple murder, Maureen Singh said, 'He were alright. He used to talk to us. He'd do anything for you, he helped us come and organise the garden, helped us move, he put panelling inside the laundry. He'd do anything for you. You can't tell me he's simple, because he's not. He's not psychiatric either, no way.'

Laurance became a regular guest at the Singh house on the outskirts of Griffith, often staying overnight.

The Griffith Schoolboy Murders

Although he had his odd ways, he was trusted by Maureen and her four children.

In the *Herald* interview Maureen Singh recalled one sinister conversation she had had with Laurance that meant nothing at the time but would explain a lot in times to come. When he said that he had done a bit of babysitting in the past, she laughed and asked him what he knew about children and said, 'How do you keep them occupied?'

Laurance explained that he played a game called 'tie-ups', where he would tie the children to a chair with rope and see how quickly they could get the rope undone. Then he would ask the children to do the same to him.

Maureen Singh said that often they would visit Laurance at home unannounced, only to find him walking around the house naked. Once, on a fishing trip to nearby Darlington Point, Laurance suddenly stripped off, ran around naked and approached her son Andrew and offered him money for sex. The teenager laughed it off as a joke, as did Laurance.

'He were a good mate of Andrew,' Maureen Singh said in the interview. 'He used to treat him real good. But it were a means to his own ends, that's why he was good to us. He were after Andrew.'

In December 1983, Laurance moved into a flat at the rear of a large family house that had been converted into apartments at 22 Yarrabee Street, near the Griffith Showground. His landlord, Merv Platt, who lived in the front of the house, described him as a quiet and tidy tenant who paid his rent on time. When Laurance wasn't doing charity work for the Smith Family, he was helping his neighbour,

Michael George Laurance

the landlord's 82-year-old sister, Aunt Molly, in her garden.

'He was a loner; he ran his own race,' Merv Platt told the *Herald*. 'But there was nothing in his behaviour which struck me as odd or unusual. He didn't appear to drink. He was just a normal person as far as I knew.'

Aunt Molly was even more impressed with the man who would soon bury a young boy's corpse in her backyard. 'Butter wouldn't melt in his mouth,' she told *The Sydney Morning Herald*. 'I trusted him. That's how good he was. He acted so naturally. He was neat and clean, courteous and well-spoken, and would often come in for a cup of tea and a chat.'

But the peaceful times were about to come to an abrupt end.

On Saturday, 29 September 1984, Laurance lured two boys into his flat. Once inside, he sexually molested and murdered them.

Twelve-year-old Mark Mott and his 11-year-old mate, Ralph Burns, had had a terrific day together at the Griffith Show with the $10 that Mark's mum had saved and given him to spend and the $20 donated by Ralph's grandfather, 'Bronco' Burns, who had raised the lad since his (Ralph's) mother committed suicide three years earlier.

It was true that both boys had more of a free spirit than most other kids their age, and were more at home sitting on the bank of a river fishing or participating in adventures than sitting in a schoolroom.

Laurance would later tell police that as the boys were making their way home from the Griffith Show down Yarrabee Street that afternoon, they passed Laurance's residence, which was only a few hundred

The Griffith Schoolboy Murders

metres from the showground. Laurance lured the boys inside and killed them.

That night Michael Laurance buried Ralph Burns in his backyard and Mark Mott in the backyard of his trusting neighbour, Aunt Molly. Some time later, Laurance dug the bodies up and dumped them at nearby Lake Wyangan. Mark Mott's remains were found in the water almost 12 months after the boys went missing. Ralph Burns's remains were found in the area by a rabbit shooter three months after Motts's body was found. They were hidden under a bush.

At the time the lads went missing, there was not a reason on earth for police to suspect that Laurance had anything to do with their disappearance, and with no leads and no bodies, the grief-stricken families of the boys had to be content with the local theory that the two free-spirited youths had run away together on an adventure and would turn up somewhere down the track.

Meanwhile, Laurance's relationship with his landlord, Merv Platt, and with Aunt Molly, came to an abrupt halt one afternoon when they arrived home to find their houses under siege and Laurance holding the police at bay with a gun.

He had bailed the police up with they arrived to question him about allegations that he had been exposing himself to schoolchildren while clad only in a balaclava. Police subdued Laurance and took him away after he had taken an overdose of pills in an attempt at suicide.

Released on bail, Laurance was evicted from his flat and took up residence in a tiny shack on the edge of an isolated fruit farm at Hanwood, a village about 7 km from Griffith.

Michael George Laurance

While working on a construction site in Griffith in 1986, Albury bricklaying contractor Peter Purtell became friendly with some of the locals and arranged for his son's Under 8 team to come across and play the Griffith side.

In a strange twist of fate, Laurance was working as an air-conditioning labourer at the same construction site at the time, though he and Purtell had little contact.

As he did every Saturday, Michael Laurance attended the junior football match to watch the Albury Under 8s, captained by 8-year-old John Purtell, Peter Purtell's son, win their game.

In the change rooms after the game, Laurance approached John Purtell and offered to wring out his underpants. The boy trustingly gave them to him, then Laurance waited outside until the boy came out and lured him back to his shack. He sexually abused the boy and eventually murdered him and hid his body.

Thanks to observant bystanders who were in the change rooms on the day John Purtell went missing, an identikit drawing of an incredible likeness to Laurance was made up and circulated. Within days, it led police to the pederast's door.

At first Laurance denied any knowledge of the disappearance of John Purtell, but when police called again five days later, after Laurance had made yet another suicide attempt, he confessed to abducting and murdering the missing boy and took police to his body, which he had concealed under a log at Darlington Point, a popular fishing spot on the Murrumbidgee River, 30 km from Griffith.

Then Laurance told police, 'Poor little Burnsey and Motty. I killed them too.' He also showed police a

The Griffith Schoolboy Murders

secret compartment in his dining table that concealed albums full of photos of naked boys, newspaper cuttings of boys missing and presumed dead and items which showed his preoccupation with skeletons and death.

Michael George Laurance made a full confession and told in graphic detail of the unimaginable horror he subjected his young victims to as he sexually abused and murdered them.

Laurance told police that on the afternoon that Ralph Burns and Mark Mott disappeared, he had spotted them coming down Yarrabee Street and had enticed them into his flat by telling them that they could come in and play games.

One of the games was called 'tie-up'. Once the boys were inside, the persuasive Laurance secured them with ropes in such a fashion that they couldn't untie themselves and then he abused them in front of each other.

'We played tie-ups and when I tied them up I got very sexually excited,' he said. Laurance then told police that he carried Ralph Burns into the bathroom and drowned him in the bathtub and put the body in the wardrobe before drowning Mark Mott.

'I put Burns in the bath and was drowning him and while I was drowning him I was also playing with his penis,' he told stunned police. 'I held his head under the water and then, when the bubbles stopped and he stopped kicking, I lifted him out of the bathtub, undone the ropes, carried him in and put him in the wardrobe.'

'I carried Mark Mott into the shower room and also played with him while I was drowning him. I wanted to stop but I could not, I was so sexually excited. It gave me a thrill watching them die. I got an erection watching them drown in the bathtub.'

Laurance then told of how he had buried their bodies in the backyard and next door and dug them up and disposed of them later.

In the interview, Laurance said he went to the shower block on the afternoon of 21 June 1986 and watched some boys showering. He offered to dry out the underpants of two boys.

When John Purtell left the shower, Laurance followed him outside and asked him if he would like a hamburger. Purtell went with him and he then drove home to Hanwood, telling the boy he had to feed the cats.

'I just wanted a boy,' Laurance said. 'Young boys just turn me on.'

'At home I played with him and then taped his hands in front of him and then played with him again.'

Laurance then put the boy in the back of his car and drove to Darlington Point, where he played with the boy again. Laurance allegedly said that when the boy 'started to scream and kick', he taped his mouth and also the boy's nose with 'wide' tape.

When Purtell died, Laurance hid the body beneath a tree trunk.

At his trial in September 1987, Laurance pleaded not guilty to murder due to a mental condition which diminished his capacity to understand and control his actions.

The jury didn't believe the defence and took only half an hour to find Laurance guilty of murdering the three boys.

The Griffith Schoolboy Murders

In sentencing Laurance, Justice Slattery said his 'crimes were such that he should not hold out any hope of ever being released from custody'.

'The prisoner carried out these dreadful deeds in a cruel, cold-blooded and unemotional state without any mercy or apparent feeling whatsoever for his young and helpless victims,' the judge said.

'Laurance's claim that he invited Mott and Burns into his flat was unlikely. It is more likely that he met the boys elsewhere, possibly at the Griffith Show, and lured them into his flat for sexual gratification.'

As the judge spoke, Laurance sat in the dock, appearing as emotionless as he had seemed for the duration of the week-long trial.

'After sexually abusing each boy,' Justice Slattery continued, 'Laurance drowned them one at a time in his bathtub after realising his identification and subsequent detection were almost certain.'

'While [Burns] witnessed the bath being run, his last minutes alive must have been appalling. Mott, tied up in the lounge room, would probably have been aware of what happened to his companion and of his own likely fate. They too must have been terrible moments for him.'

Of John Purtell, the third murdered boy, the judge said, in reference to some cotton found in the boy's throat at the post-mortem: 'The prisoner probably placed a ball of cotton wool in his mouth to stop him screaming. He then taped his mouth and nose, well knowing that the boy would die.'

'Bound, gagged and taped, the boy subsequently died. It is hard to imagine a more cruel or callous act. There is only one sentence for a person who has

Michael George Laurance

perpetrated such terrible crimes on young boys and that is life imprisonment, which I now impose.'

Justice Slattery continued: 'While acknowledging that it is not binding on the executive or parole authorities, nevertheless, having presided over this trial, it is my opinion and my recommendation that the prisoner should never be released into the community.'

At 8.40 am on 16 November 1995, Michael George Laurance was found dead, hanging from the bars of the window in his cell at Lithgow prison. At a coronial inquest held on 29 April 1996, it was concluded that he committed suicide.

Chapter 6

STANLEY BRIAN TAYLOR

The Russell Street Bomber

The four men accused of bombing the Russell Street police station in 1986 were 'rapt' when they saw the bomb explode, and disappointed that it only killed one police officer, the Melbourne Supreme Court was told at their trial.

The court was also told that one of the accused, Rodney Minogue, believed they should have parked the car beneath the building, 'which would have brought the whole building down and got more of the dogs'.

Another of the men accused of planting the bomb, Stanley Brian Taylor, was alleged to have said to a Crown witness that 'if he had a terminal illness he would strap himself up with explosives, go to Russell Street police complex and position himself to kill as many police as possible'.

Such was Stan Taylor's hatred of police. It was a hatred that would lead to the death of a young policewoman – Angela Taylor, 22 – and give Taylor the dubious honour of becoming the first prisoner in modern Victorian history to be incarcerated without the possibility of parole.

Charged with Taylor, 51 (at the time of the trial in April 1988), were Peter Michael Reed, 30, Craig

Stanley Brian Taylor

William Minogue, 25, and his brother Rodney, 22, who was described by a senior detective as having the IQ of an indoor plant. All pleaded not guilty.

The court heard that the four men allegedly planted a bomb containing 50–60 sticks of gelignite in a stolen Commodore, and left the Commodore outside the Russell Street police complex. It had exploded just after 1 pm on 27 March 1986, the day before Good Friday, at a time when the street was teeming with people. The bomb had been 'tragically, devastatingly effective' – it hurled debris more than 100 metres, some of it landing on surrounding rooftops.

'The explosion produced horrifying injuries to a young policewoman, Angela Taylor, who had been on duty at the court and was crossing the road during her lunch break', the court was told. Angela Taylor, the dux of her police academy class, died 24 days later. The bomb also injured 21 other people.

Task Force Operation Russell, consisting of 30 police, was formed to investigate this blatant act of terrorism against the Victorian police.

Acting on a tip-off that a woman had seen a man making a bomb on his kitchen table the day before the bombing, police raided a house in Broadmeadows and apprehended Claudio Crupi, a known criminal who had once fired shots at police.

On the day of the bombing, Crupi was known to have left his home about midday and returned about one hour after the bombing. When asked about the bomb he was building, Crupi said that it was a fake and that he was building it to frighten the Flemington police.

Crupi made no bones about the fact that he hated the police, the Russell Street police in particular. Police

The Russell Street Bomber

believed they had their man, but they couldn't charge Crupi because all they had was circumstantial evidence, and that would surely be beaten in court.

As it turned out, Crupi had nothing to do with the Russell Street bombing.

During the investigation into the bombing, an observant detective from the stolen car squad noticed that the car used had had its chassis number drilled off. So had another car, which had been used in an armed bank robbery in Donvale on the day of the explosion. It was a technique that known car thief Peter Reed specialised in.

Police decided to pay Reed a visit on Anzac Day, 1986. They were met with gunshots, which resulted in one of the detectives being wounded. Police shot and wounded Reed and took him into custody.

At Reed's house police found vital evidence that linked Reed and an associate, Craig Minogue, to the bombing. This led them to Stan Taylor, the alleged leader of a gang of young crooks who had graduated from car stealing to armed hold-ups under his guidance.

In the '60s, Taylor had robbed seven banks in five days, helped lead riots inside Pentridge's H Division, escaped twice and been recaptured. When he was released in 1978, after 17 years in jail, he became a mentor for wayward, unemployed young people.

On the surface, Taylor was a reformed man, but he was really a vicious robber who had an almost uncontrollable hatred of the police.

His associate, Peter Reed, wasn't much better. Police described him as the most vicious and violent member of the gang, a man who had tried to sexually humiliate

Stanley Brian Taylor

female robbery victims. Reed also hated police with a passion. He blamed them for arranging for his mother to be given injections which sent her insane.

Taylor was also a 'dog' (informer). When he was arrested, he admitted his involvement in a recent spate of armed robberies, including the one at Donvale on the day of the bombing, in which shots were fired. But he steadfastly denied any involvement in the Russell Street bombing. Instead, he implicated the members of his gang.

Taylor said that he knew Reed and Craig Minogue were going to commit the crime and he confronted them about it. Yet only hours after the bombing, he had committed the Donvale armed robbery with the same men.

In his statement, Taylor said that on the day of the blast, he saw a car loaded with gelignite, and Reed in frenzy saying, 'We've got to go.' Taylor said he refused to participate in the bombing. When the group returned, he told them he had seen a news report about a gas explosion in the city. Reed had replied, 'Bullshit. That was us.'

Taylor said the other three monitored television and radio stations to hear about the explosion. 'In my opinion, they were getting off on the broadcasts,' Taylor said.

Taylor maintained his innocence to the last, saying, 'I am not a murderer, never have been, never will be. I am no more a murderer than a football follower who shouts out to kill the umpire [is a murderer].'

Police alleged that it was Reed's idea to bomb the police station, that Taylor helped build the crude bomb with a simple alarm clock device, and that Craig

Minogue and his younger brother Rodney also participated.

The jury didn't believe Taylor, and he was convicted of the murder of policewoman Angela Taylor and of a series of armed robberies. He was sentenced to life imprisonment, with no fixed non-parole period.

Craig William Minogue was found guilty of the murder of Angela Taylor and sentenced to life imprisonment with a minimum non-parole period of 28 years. Minogue was also sentenced to 14 years for the armed robberies and to 27 years for killing Alex Tsakmakis, in Pentridge's H Division.

Peter Michael Reed was acquitted of the bombing, though police still maintain that he planned it. Reed was acquitted of the attempted murder of the detective he shot on the Anzac Day raid on his house but was convicted of the attempted murder of another detective who was standing beside the wounded officer. Reed was also convicted of armed robbery and wrongful imprisonment, and sentenced to 13 years for the attempted murder and 12 years for the armed robberies.

Rodney Patrick Minogue was convicted of being an accessory to the bombing but was later acquitted on appeal. He was sentenced to 8 years for armed robbery.

Chapter 7

ROBERT RAYMOND DAY

The Japanese Tourist Murder Mystery

When 37-year-old Brisbane labourer Robert Raymond Day was found guilty in 1990 in the Brisbane Supreme Court of the attempted murder of a Danish tourist, Hendrik Enevoldsen, in December 1988, and sentenced to life imprisonment, the sentencing judge added what seemed to be a particularly harsh recommendation for the crime, considering that no one had been murdered.

Justice Shepherdson said that a psychiatric report labelled Day as being capable of extremely violent behaviour, a 'dangerous man', and that there was an extremely high risk that he would re-offend in the same manner.

The judge ordered that jail authorities be informed of these remarks, and that they take note of them at all times 'for the protection of fellow prisoners', and that this should apply anywhere that Day was likely to be imprisoned in the future.

Justice Shepherdson told Day that there was really only one sentence he could impose – life – and that he should not be released from custody at any time. His papers should be marked 'never to be released'.

Japanese Tourist Murder Mystery

They were harsh words indeed, possibly the harshest ever uttered by a sentencing judge in Queensland, especially for *attempted* murder, but a closer look into the circumstances leading up to Justice Shepherdson's recommendation reveals that the judge was basing his recommendation on far more than just the attempted murder conviction.

On 23 December 1988, Day appeared in the Cleveland Magistrates' Court charged with the attempted murder of 21-year-old Hendrik Enevoldsen. Then on 30 December 1988, Day was charged in the Brisbane Magistrates' Court with the murder of a Japanese tourist, Noriyuki Oda, 22, who was last seen buying tickets for a bus trip to Alice Springs at the Brisbane Transit Centre on 4 December.

Day entered no plea to charges of attempted murder, murder, and assaulting a police officer, and was remanded in custody. On 26 May, back in the Brisbane Magistrates' Court, it was alleged that homicide detectives had found Japanese-brand items, including shampoo, conditioner, tissues and a pen, in a flat used by Day.

A friend of Noriyuki Oda who was flown in from Japan as a witness identified the pen as similar to one she had given to Oda in a KFC outlet where they worked together in Japan.

The witness also identified an unusual brand of tissues found at Day's apartment as the same brand she had sold Oda before he left for Australia. Police also found an Oriental amulet, alleged to have been Oda's, in a rubbish bin at Day's flat. And a pair of handcuffs.

The man Day was alleged to have attempted to murder, Hendrik Enevoldsen, told the court that he had travelled with Day from the Brisbane Transit Centre to Redland Bay. There Day allegedly attacked him from behind with a piece of timber while he was taking pictures of a hollow tree near a bushland swamp, then tried to drown him in the swamp. Enevoldsen escaped and flagged down a passing motorist.

Day was committed for trial for the murder of Noriyuki Oda and the attempted murder of Hendrik Enevoldsen.

At his trial for the murder of Oda, in the Brisbane Supreme Court, it was alleged that Day had not only confessed the murder to two Brisbane jail inmates, but had also asked one of them who was about to be released if he could murder another Japanese for him in order to help his (Day's) defence case.

Day allegedly told the two men that he had handcuffed Oda to a tree, poured petrol at his feet, then taunted him by saying 'you burn, you burn' as he set him ablaze. Day was then alleged to have concealed Mr Oda's body in a 44-gallon drum containing chemicals and buried it.

After 20 days in court, hearing from 20 witnesses, including 13 flown in from Japan, the trial was aborted. In discharging the jury, Justice Shepherdson said that he was mindful of the hundreds of thousands of dollars in costs incurred already, but if he allowed the case to continue he would be left with a strong sense of having treated Day unfairly.

Justice Shepherdson had ruled that a Japanese handwriting expert could only give evidence on a narrow basis – comparison between Japanese characters on documents accepted as Oda's and those on a cassette case found in Day's flat.

Japanese Tourist Murder Mystery

The expert had gone further in his evidence, and Bill Cuthbert, counsel for Day, had submitted that his case was now prejudiced because he could not cross-examine on evidence that the judge had ruled inadmissible but that the jury had inadvertently heard. The judge agreed, and thus the trial was aborted.

Day was retried for Oda's murder in June 1990, and was acquitted. But he remained in custody to face the attempted murder charge.

On 1 November 1990, Day was found guilty of the attempted murder of Hendrik Enevoldsen. Justice Shepherdson said that he was concerned about similarities between the evidence presented about the death of Noriyuki Oda and that presented in the attempted murder case.

'I heard sworn testimony in that [the Oda death] trial that certainly suggested this man killed the Japanese man Oda,' Justice Shepherdson said. 'I realise that Day had been acquitted, but what concerned me is [that] this offence involving Enevoldsen occurred two to three weeks after Oda disappeared when, it was said in Oda's case, the accused had killed him.'

On 7 December 1990, Day was sent to prison with his papers marked 'never to be released'.

In the psychiatric report that played such an important role in the sentencing of Day, it was revealed that at the age of 18, Day had entered a block of flats at Spring Hill one afternoon and, at knifepoint, raped a 55-year-old crippled woman.

Day had attacked and sexually assaulted the woman as she was crawling across the floor of her apartment to change the channel on the television set. Day served 11 years for this crime, and was released in 1982.

Robert Raymond Day

On 8 April 1993, the remains of Noriyuki Oda were found in a bush grave in the Beerburrum state forest on the Sunshine Coast. Oda had died from severe head injuries administered by an 'instrument of some kind'.

This leaves the riddle: did Day lie about how he had killed Oda and dispose of his body? Perhaps, in fact, he knew nothing about Mr Oda's death at all, and the jury at his second trial was right.

But then again, Robert Raymond Day could have carried out the perfect murder – and got away with it.

Perhaps we will never know. Day still maintains that he is innocent of the murder of Noriyuki Oda.

Chapter 8

RODNEY FRANCIS CAMERON

The Lonely Hearts Killer

After being found guilty of the serial murders of a man and a woman in 1974, Rodney Francis Cameron was described by psychiatrists as having an 'extreme psychopathic personality' and as being 'not fit to be in society'.

Cameron was sentenced to be kept behind bars 'for the term of his natural life'. Incredibly, he would be released 16 years after he committed the murders, and would kill again.

According to court records, Cameron was born in Kew, Victoria, shortly after his father died. One of his earliest recollections was watching his mother drop dead in front of him as she pulled a cake from the oven.

As a 7-year-old, now adopted, Cameron was continually in trouble at school for attacking little girls. Soon after, he was committed to an institution – after he endangered passengers' lives by placing boxes on a railway line, in the path of oncoming trains – prompting a psychiatrist to say at the time that he considered that there was 'no therapy available that would be of use to him'.

At 10, Cameron tried to strangle a little girl. She survived the vicious assault. He also jumped on, and

Rodney Francis Cameron

tried to strangle, an elderly lady in the street, and attempted to throttle a girlfriend in his early adult years.

By that time, Cameron's adoptive family had completely rejected him.

By his late teens, Cameron had started drinking heavily and taking heroin and morphine. He also attempted suicide on numerous occasions, dabbled in devil worship, the occult and demonology, and openly displayed hostility and extreme aggression toward those close to him, particularly those who had shown him any form of kindness.

Something was about to give ... and it did.

On 31 January 1974, the then 19-year-old Cameron claimed his first victim – nurse Florence Edith Jackson, 49. He raped and murdered her at her Katoomba home after she had befriended him at the Queen Victoria Nursing Home at nearby Wentworth Falls, where he worked as a trainee nurse.

Cameron had strangled his friend into unconsciousness, then raped her, then strangled her again until she stopped breathing. Miss Jackson was left lying on her back beside the bed with a towel stuffed down her throat.

Inserting cloth items down the victims' throats after death would become the serial killer's calling card.

A week later, at Mallacoota, in Victoria, Cameron committed a second murder. He bashed 19-year-old bank clerk Francesco Ciliberto with a boulder and then strangled him with a football sock. Ciliberto had picked Cameron up while he was hitchhiking south toward Victoria.

The dead man was later found lying on his back with a shirt stuffed down his throat.

The Lonely Hearts Killer

Cameron was arrested in Queensland on 21 February 1974 after he abducted a mother and daughter. Cameron told arresting police that he 'had to kill three'.

Cameron was tried in NSW for the murder of Florence Jackson and served 9 years jail. The trial was a history-making event in that Cameron tried to plead guilty to manslaughter, instead of murder, on the grounds of diminished responsibility. This was the first time such a defence had ever been used in a murder trial. It failed, and he was convicted of murder.

In 1983, Cameron was released and immediately extradited to Victoria to face the charge of murdering Francesco Ciliberto. At his trial he was diagnosed as an 'extreme psychopath', and it was recommended by the judge that Cameron should remain in jail 'for the term of his natural life' for the brutal murder of the young man who had been kind enough to give him a lift and had paid for it with his life.

It seemed that Cameron had at last been recognised for what he was, a psychopathic serial killer, and had been put away for good, unable to hurt more innocent citizens.

But that was not to be. In what would prove to be one of the greatest blunders ever perpetrated by a parole board, a blunder that would cost the life of at least one more innocent victim (and possibly another four), Cameron was released back into society on 12 March 1990, after successfully appealing in November 1989 against the length of his sentence. It was said at the time that he was thought to be fully rehabilitated.

He had married his lifelong friend, Anne, in jail in 1986 and had apparently settled down to a quiet domestic life in Sunbury, northwest of Melbourne, where he landed (with the help of forged references) a good job as the live-in manager of a stud farm. But this life was not to last.

On a match-making show on radio 3AW in Melbourne on 26 May 1990, Cameron described himself as a non-smoking, non-drinking, Gemini marine biologist from Castlemaine who had no hang-ups, liked squash and basketball and was searching for a partner 'willing to share his happiness and enjoy a good, quiet life'.

Less than a month later, on 23 June, at the Sky Rider Motor Inn in Katoomba (in the Blue Mountains, just outside Sydney), a 44-year-old Melbourne woman, Maria Goeliner, was found on her back with a handkerchief stuffed in her mouth. The handkerchief was secured by a pair of pantyhose wrapped around her neck. There was a bunch of yellow carnations lying on her body.

Maria Goeliner, the unluckiest of nine lonely women who had rung the program expressing an interest in meeting Cameron, had died of asphyxiation, choking on her own blood after being repeatedly bashed over the head with a blunt instrument. There was also evidence of strangulation.

Maria Goeliner was described by those who knew her as a loving, trusting person. She was looking for someone she could settle down with when she rang the match-making program. Instead, Maria Goeliner wound up with a psychopathic murderer who had just been released after 16 years' imprisonment.

The couple had arrived two days earlier and paid for two days' accommodation in advance. They

The Lonely Hearts Killer

had requested a 'do not disturb' sign on bungalow number 46.

On Friday 22 June, about lunchtime, motel staff had seen Maria Goeliner and Cameron together. This was quite possibly the last time she was ever seen alive.

The next morning, the manager delivered their ordered breakfast and, when no one responded, left the tray inside the door. Finding the meal untouched later, the cleaner investigated and found Maria Goeliner on the floor in the bathroom.

In the room was a note from Cameron to his wife, Anne, which read in part: 'Anne, I am sorry. Had I not done what happened, my life would have been destroyed. Love eternally, Rodney.'

Police had no problems fitting the missing man's description to Cameron. And the murder was chillingly similar to the killer's two previous slayings in 1974.

A week after the murder, Cameron gave himself up to police at Deniliquin in NSW, claiming that a mysterious 'second man' named Frederick Mulner had travelled with him and Maria, and it was Mulner who had committed the murder.

Giving him the benefit of the doubt, police searched electoral rolls, phone books, birth and death records, police records – every possible avenue available – for the missing Mulner.

Of course, the mysterious Frederick Mulner was never found – he almost certainly didn't exist.

Cameron was described by the arresting officers at Deniliquin, Pat English and Steve McGlynn, as like no other murderer they had ever met. 'To see him, to hear him, you would say he's a politely spoken, neatly dressed, quiet sort of a guy. To realise what he's capable of doing is quite scary. He really shows no compassion,' they said.

'He is calculating and cunning. We regard him as the most dangerous man you would probably ever meet.'

As his trial for murdering Florence Edith Jackson was back in 1974, Cameron's trial in October 1992 was also an extraordinary event, in that the Crown was allowed to bring up Cameron's past murders.

The jury members, far from being protected from knowledge of his previous crimes in case the information prejudiced them against the defendant, were given every grim detail about Cameron's horrific past offences.

It was the first time that 'similar fact' evidence had been used in a murder trial in NSW this century, and the Crown prosecutor, Barry Newport, QC, went to great lengths to explain to the jury how they could treat the knowledge that Cameron was a convicted double murderer.

'It would be wrong,' he said, 'to say: Well, that's it. He has killed twice before, therefore he did it this time. But it could be used to exclude the possibility that Frederick Mulner was the killer. After all, how extraordinary it would be if this mystery (person) should be there and the mystery (person) should kill in a fashion so similar to the way in which the accused had killed twice in the past.'

Only the jury will ever know how they interpreted the evidence, but it only took them three hours to find Rodney Francis Cameron, now dubbed the 'Lonely Hearts Killer', guilty of the murder of Maria Goeliner.

In passing the strongest possible sentence – life imprisonment with the recommendation that he is 'never to be released' – Justice Newman said that only 'old age or infirmity' would ever stop Cameron from trying to fulfil his 'homicidal desires'.

On 20 April 1993, police charged Cameron with the brutal murder of 79-year-old Sydney pensioner, Sarah McKenzie, almost two decades earlier.

On 6 February 1974, Mrs McKenzie had phoned police from her home to report that she had been bashed by a man, but when police arrived, the house was locked up and there was no sign of life.

Police returned to the house two days later and broke in. They found Mrs McKenzie's body in the hallway with 30 knife wounds to her chest, a knife embedded in her neck and a mattock buried in her skull.

Police had discovered that while on the run after murdering Francesco Ciliberto in 1974, Cameron had been booked for speeding in Ciliberto's car at Nowra, in southern NSW. The same car had been reported by a highway patrol officer at North Sydney about the same time on the day Mrs McKenzie was believed to have been bashed to death.

The highway patrol officer had found Cameron asleep in the car on the expressway and had questioned him about being in the area.

Police had re-opened the McKenzie murder file after hearing from jail informers that Cameron had been boasting of his past crimes. Cameron strongly denied the allegations, and three days before the trial was to begin, in early 1994, it was no-billed by the NSW Department of Public Prosecutions (not proceeded with because there is a lack of conclusive admissible evidence, or where the case against the defendant is not sufficiently strong as to give good prospects of success).

Rodney Francis Cameron

On 3 October 1997, the now 42-year-old Cameron requested through prison officials at Lithgow Correctional Centre to speak to police, and in a lengthy, videotaped confession told Northern Region Homicide and North Sydney detectives that he did in fact kill Mrs McKenzie. He supplied them with details only the killer could have known.

Later, Cameron also confessed to Melbourne police that he murdered two women in separate knife attacks in Victoria in 1990, and was also ready to confess to bashing in a man's skull in 1974 in South Australia, and the strangulation murder of a woman in NSW in the same year.

'I've got to get all this off my chest,' Cameron was reported to have said to a friend. 'I know I'll rot in jail, but I want to clear the slate.'

He is also reported to have blamed his heavy indulgence in hallucinogenic drugs in the early 1970s for his blood lust. 'I was into satanism and taking drugs. I didn't know where I was,' he allegedly told the friend.

If Cameron's confessions are proven to be correct, this would bring the number of his victims to eight, making him the most prolific serial killer in Australia's history, with one more victim than Backpacker Killer Ivan Milat.

But for the time being, Rodney Francis Cameron is in maximum security in Lithgow prison, 'never to be released'.

Chapter 9

ANDREW PETER GARFORTH

Ebony: The Murder of Ebony Simpson

They say that out of all evil comes some good. But there was a time when you would have had a hard time convincing Christine and Peter Simpson that any good could possibly come out of the murder of their beloved daughter, Ebony.

But it did. Left alone with their two teenage sons, Zac and Tas, in their unimaginable grief after Ebony's murder, the Simpson family wondered why no one came near them, why no one counselled them, why they were so alone in their hour of desperate need.

As they would find out later, it was because people didn't know how to handle the situation, and rather than impose on them, and possibly say the wrong thing, people stayed away.

And at the time of Ebony's murder in 1992, there were no counsellors who specialised in the needs of those left behind when someone is suddenly taken from them through homicide.

The Simpsons' desperate need for a shoulder to lean on led to the formation of the Homicide Victims' Support Group (HVSG), which now has branches in almost every State of Australia helping normal,

Andrew Peter Garforth

everyday people come to terms with having a loved one murdered.

It is impossible to imagine how to cope with the murder of a family member or friend. Only someone who has experienced it can relate to it, and that is wherethe HVSG comes in. They can provide love, kindness and understanding, because they too are people who have experienced the heartbreak of losing a loved one to homicide.

The HVSG also fights vigorously for its members, campaigning for increased rights for the victims left behind, harsher sentences for the perpetrators of the crimes and greater community and government awareness of the plight of the loved ones left in the wake of murder.

Yes, it would be fair to say that some good did come out of the evil that happened on that horrible day in 1992. Ebony Simpson's death was not in vain.

When 9-year-old Ebony Simpson alighted from the school bus at 4.05 pm on Wednesday, 19 August 1992, on the corner of Bargo and Arina Roads in Bargo, the tiny rural town (population 2935) situated in the NSW southern highlands, to walk the 400 metres to her home, the last thing on her mind would have been that someone was waiting to abduct, sexually assault and murder her.

But a predator was waiting. It was Andrew Peter Garforth, 29, a short, thin man with dirty, shoulder-length mousy-coloured hair and pale blue eyes. Garforth was an unemployed labourer who lived at nearby Pheasants Nest and was the father of two young boys.

As Ebony Simpson walked towards her house along Arina Road, she came across Garforth as he stood

The Murder of Ebony Simpson

beside his car. The bonnet was up and the boot was open. As she approached the car, Garforth bundled her into the boot, dropped the bonnet and took off to a dirt track in Charles Point Road, Bargo, and from there to a dam 7 km away.

Parked near the water's edge, Garforth removed the terrified child from the boot of the car and sat her on the front seat with him. She pleaded not to be harmed and to be released. But instead, Garforth took Ebony from the car to the edge of the dam. He bound her feet together and her hands behind her back with speaker wire and sexually abused her.

Then Garforth threw the girl, still bound, into the dam, along with her school bag (which he weighed down with rocks). He walked away, ignoring her pleas for help, and drove home.

The following day, at the instigation of his de facto wife Denise, the mother of his two sons (aged one and three), Garforth joined in the search for the missing girl along with 150 other volunteers including police, bushfire brigade and State Emergency Services volunteers, trail bike riders and local residents.

The only clue that police had was the description of a man in his late twenties who was seen working on an early model light-coloured Mazda near the bus stop where Ebony disappeared.

Police described the car as being in poor condition, with smoke stains from the exhaust all over the back. It had been seen several times in the vicinity of primary and high schools in the district over the past months.

One local reported that the same car had been sighted following school buses. The man driving it was described as being about 177 cm tall, with straight

Andrew Peter Garforth

brown shoulder-length hair, a thin build, and wearing a black, long-sleeved top and black jeans.

Answering the description perfectly, Garforth was picked up by police while driving a car answering the description of the car seen near Ebony Simpson's home on the day she disappeared.

Admitting his guilt, Garforth took police divers to where he had left Ebony Simpson to drown. Her body was recovered at 12.45 am on Friday, 21 August.

Garforth was charged with murder and made a full confession, in which he described how he abducted, tied up, and sexually assaulted Ebony Simpson, then threw her, alive, into the dam and left her to die.

Hardened police were horrified at Garforth's lack of remorse as he told of the terrifying last moments of Ebony Simpson's life. When asked what happened when he threw Ebony in the dam, Garforth told police: 'Shouted help.'

'What did you do then?'

'I walked away. When I left her she was trying to get back to the bank.'

'Did you think she would die?'

'I believed that she could have possibly drowned or maybe made it to the bank.'

Garforth appeared in a packed Picton Courthouse on 21 August 1992, charged with the murder of Ebony Simpson. As he was led from the police cells next door, his head covered by a white towel and wearing jeans and a leather jacket, an outraged crowd of around 200, some of them openly weeping, yelled abuse and hurled missiles.

In the dock, Garforth remained emotionless and hung his head as the police prosecutor outlined the allegations to the magistrate.

The Murder of Ebony Simpson

Garforth pleaded guilty to murdering Ebony Simpson, and at his sentencing on 9 July 1993 at the Darlinghurst Supreme Court, the crowded courtroom erupted as Justice Newman handed down the maximum sentence – life imprisonment – under the NSW truth-in-sentencing legislation, meaning that Garforth would never be released. Justice Newman said that the case 'does fall squarely into the category of the worst type of case'.

It was only the fifth time that such a sentence had been handed down since the introduction of the legislation in 1989.

In his summing up, Justice Newman made scathing comments about Garforth, and did little to hold back his contempt. Justice Newman said he believed Garforth's attitude to the crime was best reflected by his 'almost casual' answers in the interviews and that his lack of remorse after arrest was 'a matter of gravity'.

'Garforth's comment about what he expected the girl to do after he threw her, tied up, in the dam, was chilling in the extreme,' he said. 'The callous indifference to the fate of his victim by the prisoner would appal any civilised human being.'

The judge said that drowning 'is a terrifying and slow manner of death' and the little girl's 'last moments must have been spent in abject fear'.

'This is not a case where his intention was to cause grievous bodily harm to his victim. His intention was to kill.'

Responding to a defence submission that Garforth was entitled to leniency due to the fact that he had been co-operative with police by taking them to the murder scene and then pleading guilty, Justice Newman responded by saying, 'This is a case where the prisoner literally had no defence and no chance of finding one. I consider the sexual assault and the girl's fear as aggravating features in the highest degree.'

Justice Newman took into account the fact that if Garforth lived to the average age of males of the time, he could expect to spend 42 years behind bars, and as a child murderer in protective custody, he could expect that his time would be 'more arduous' than usual.

'The imposition of a life sentence is not a matter that this court would take lightly,' Justice Newman concluded.

After the sentencing, Ebony's father, Peter Simpson, applauded the sentence and made this heart-wrenching statement to the press.

I'd like to say I'm happy with the decision. It's taken nearly 11 long months to see justice served and this is the best outcome we could possibly hope for under the present legal system in this State of NSW in 1993.

The fact remains that Ebony Simpson got the death sentence, the Simpson family got the life sentence and Garforth got bed and breakfast. The murderer's been given the very minimum that he deserves, a life sentence. He has shown no remorse, no shame and no feeling. This man has no soul.

He abducted, tortured, sexually abused, murdered and discarded our beautiful Ebony in such a cruel and malicious way. How could anyone be sure he would not murder again?

Garforth's selfish, barbaric, murderous act has had a profound effect on so many people's lives, the ramifications of which may never really be known. Ebony's murder need never be forgotten. Ebony's death was untimely, unnecessary and senseless. It has thrown my family, myself into a nightmare existence.

The Murder of Ebony Simpson

This man has done the ultimate robbery. He has robbed our dear Ebony of 70 years of her life, Chris and I of our daughter and Zac and Tas of their lovely sister. Living without Ebony is like living without the sun – every day is overcast. Learning to live without Ebony is like learning to live with an amputation. You never ever get the limb back, you just learn to live without it. Our life is like a jigsaw puzzle with one piece always missing.

No, this murderer should never be allowed back in society ever again under any circumstance. This man has a lot to answer for. Even though the trial is over for most people, for the Simpson family it's just the tip of the iceberg.'

In 1994, the Simpson family won the Good Citizen Awards category in the International Year of the Family awards.

Life in prison and on the appeals front has been anything but pleasant for Andrew Peter Garforth. As a child-killer, he has been and always will be a target for other prisoners.

Shortly after he was charged in August 1992, Garforth was attacked at the Long Bay Remand Centre while he was alone in a locked holding yard.

A prison spokesperson said that despite extra precautions taken by prison guards to keep an eye on Garforth, a large group of prisoners in an adjoining area suddenly lunged towards Garforth and broke the lock on his door.

In October 1993, Garforth was bashed for the second time, by inmates in Goulburn Jail.

On 30 March 1994, Garforth appealed to the Supreme Court of NSW against the severity of his life

Andrew Peter Garforth

sentence, claiming that the murder of Ebony Simpson was not in the 'worst case' category.

Garforth's counsel, Martin Sides QC, argued that the crime did not fall into the class of crimes for which the life sentence (now for the term of the prisoner's natural life) was intended when it was introduced.

Mr Sides said there were other cases where victims had drowned, often slowly, that had not attracted the life penalty.

'In all of the circumstances of this case, when one approaches it in a correct fashion, this does not fall into that category of the very worst or the most heinous,' he said.

Mr Sides also said that the sentencing judge failed to give due consideration to other relevant factors, such as that Garforth pleaded guilty before his trial and made admissions to police that led them to recovering Ebony Simpson's body, which otherwise may never have been found.

On 23 May 1994, the Court of Criminal Appeal ruled that the case against Garforth was so extreme that community interest in retribution and punishment called for the maximum term.

In November 1994, Garforth gave notice that he would be appealing yet again, this time to the High Court, against his life sentence.

'How many judges do you need to say someone's guilty?' Christine Simpson told reporters. 'We've had four judges already saying it and now there will be another three. It makes a nonsense of the truth-in-sentencing legislation. Truth in sentencing was in place when we came out of court in July 1993, and that should be the end of it.

The Murder of Ebony Simpson

'Garforth says his life sentence should be reduced because he co-operated with police and told them where Ebony's body was. But police said they were going to drag the dam anyway. They would have found her because her lunch box was floating on top.

'My family is shattered at the news of the appeal. My husband will be taking time off work. He can't go through the stress of working and having to think about what's ahead.'

On 7 December 1994, Garforth's application for special leave to appeal against his life sentence was rejected by the High Court.

With all avenues of appeal now exhausted, Andrew Peter Garforth will never be released from jail.

After Ebony's death, her parents, 42-year-old housewife Christine and 44-year-old Telecom employee Peter Simpson, were angry at the lack of structured support from the community and welfare groups. No one had been to see them about putting them in touch with other families who had experienced similar tragedies and no one had contacted Ebony's school to see if any of her grieving friends needed help.

When John Merrick, head grief counsellor at the NSW Institute of Forensic Medicine, heard about the plight of the Simpson's, almost a year after Ebony's death, he visited them.

Within 24 hours, Grace and Gary Lynch had paid a follow-up visit. The Lynchs, parents of nursing sister Anita Cobby, who was murdered by five men in 1986, were well known for their support work among the relatives of crime victims.

Andrew Peter Garforth

To Merrick, his meeting with the Simpsons confirmed what he already knew – that the families and friends of homicide victims were often left to fend for themselves. So he set up the Institute of Forensic Medicine Advisory Committee and formed a board of experts comprising State Coroner Greg Glass, ex-State Coroner Kevin Waller, Gary Lynch and others.

The idea was to bring people in similar circumstances together and form an organisation to provide mutual support. With Merrick's assistant, grief counsellor Deb De Wilde, they sent 100 letters out to the families of murder victims.

Of the 35 families who responded, nine attended the first meeting, which was held in September 1993. At the next meeting, a month later, 35 people turned up, and with the support of the now Executive Director, Martha Jabour, who rang homicide victims' families to tell them of the group's progress, the numbers have since increased dramatically at each monthly meeting as the word has spread that just because you are a victim of homicide, it doesn't mean that you are alone.

Since those early days, more than 600 families have passed through the NSW HVSG.

From fledgling beginnings, the HVSG in NSW is now funded by the government to the tune of $250,000 per year, and has been directly responsible for the introduction of:

- Victim Impact Statements – the families of victims now have the right to submit a written statement to tell the court of the hardship of losing a loved one to homicide;

The Murder of Ebony Simpson

- an increase in compensation to the families from $20,000 to $50,000; and
- the Charter of Victims' Rights, which the HVSG assisted the NSW Government in drawing up.

But the ultimate compliment to the Simpson family and their beloved Ebony was the building of Ebony House, a recovery centre for the victims left behind by homicide. Ebony House was launched by the NSW Premier, Bob Carr, in 1996, and is funded by the NSW government.

Ebony House is situated in beautiful surroundings at Waterfall in Sydney's south, not far from where little Ebony's life was so tragically taken on that horrible day in 1992. It is made up of two cottages, which accommodate up to 21 people at a time. They have been used to house international guests such as the families of the German backpackers who were murdered by Ivan Milat and the families of the victims of the Dunblane School massacre in Scotland who came to Australia and were so supportive of the families of those killed in the Port Arthur massacre.

Through Ebony House and the Homicide Victims Support Groups throughout Australia, the memory of Ebony Simpson and her family will live forever. Peter Simpson was President of the NSW HVSG, and very proud of it.

Some good does come from all evil.

Chapter 10

WILLIAM PATRICK MITCHELL

The Geraldton Axe Murderer

Farmhand William Patrick Mitchell killed a mother and her two daughters and son with an axe and then had sex with one of the corpses in a house just outside of Geraldton in northern WA in February 1993. These crimes were so indecent and inhuman that he would become the first person to be put in jail in WA without the possibility of parole, without ever being able to apply to have a non-parole period set.★

Struggling to find words to describe the atrocities, Justice Neville Owen said the crimes committed by Mitchell, 24, were so serious as to 'almost defy description'. He said that Mitchell's victims were innocent and defenceless, and the killings had been accompanied by 'sexual activity of the most depraved kind'.

Mitchell had pleaded guilty to wilfully murdering Karen MacKenzie and her three children – Daniel, 16, Amara, 7, and Katrina, 5 – at the family's home near Greenough, 400 km north of Perth, on 22 February 1993. Mitchell also pleaded guilty to three counts of sexually interfering with Ms MacKenzie's corpse and the sexual penetration of her daughter, 7-year-old Amara.

The Geraldton Axe Murderer

All had been murdered with an axe. Ms MacKenzie was killed in the living room by several blows to the head. Her daughters were dressed in night clothes and were found in separate bedrooms with blows to their bodies and heads. The son's body was found outside the house with a trail of blood leading to it.

Mitchell, a farmhand, was quickly arrested, charged and pleaded guilty. Mitchell's only defence, said Robert Lindsay, acting for Mitchell, was that the killings had occurred while Mitchell was in a drug-induced frenzy and that they were motiveless and without premeditation: an acquaintance of the family, Mitchell had taken alcohol, amphetamines, analgesics and cannabis.

At Mitchell's sentencing in October 1993, Justice Owen originally chose not to make Mitchell the first person to be jailed for the term of his natural life under the new WA laws. Mr Owen instead sentenced him to life imprisonment; he would be eligible for consideration for parole in 20 years.

'I am not able to say that you will always be a danger to the public,' Justice Owen said. 'That depends on whether you stay away from drugs. If, at a time in excess of 20 years, the executive arm of the government takes the view that you do not constitute a danger to the public and are otherwise deserving of release on licence, then that is a decision that it will take.'

This decision was overturned by the full bench of the Criminal Court of Appeal in April 1994, when they ruled in a 2–1 decision that William Patrick Mitchell was too much of a risk to the community to ever be released, and recommended that he be jailed for life with no chance of parole.

William Patrick Mitchell

*Author's note: Mitchell is the first prisoner in WA to receive the maximum penalty of life without the possibility of parole under a law brought in in 1996. While other WA killers, such as David and Catherine Birnie and Darren Osborne (deceased), have been sent to prison for life with the recommendation that they never be released, under the WA law (when they were sentenced) they can still apply to have a non-parole period set after they have served a minimum of 20 years of their sentence. The Birnies, for example, are entitled to apply for parole in the year 2007.

Chapter 11

MALCOLM GEORGE BAKER

The Central Coast Massacre

It could be said that the town of Terrigal, situated on the central coast of NSW, a 60 km drive north of Sydney, is best known because it is the home of Australia's biggest-selling contemporary author, Robert G. Barrett, and was the location for the hugely successful Australian movie *Muriel's Wedding*, in which it was known as Porpoise Flats.

But while Barrett's books entertain hundreds of thousands of Australians and Muriel and her friends made us all laugh (and maybe cry), there is a dark and evil side to beautiful Terrigal.

At 10.50 on the night of 28 October 1992, 45-year-old unemployed labourer Malcolm George Baker walked into the Toukley Police Station and said that he had just murdered six people. He told them that a shotgun that he had used in the killings was in his car.

The killings had started at 9.15 that evening at a house in Barnhill Road, Terrigal, 24 km away, where Baker had shot and killed eight-months pregnant Lisa Gannan, 18, her 23-year-old sister Kerryann (Baker's ex-de facto wife), and their father, Thomas Gannan, 43, who was visiting his daughters from Sydney.

Malcolm George Baker

He also shot Kerryann's new boyfriend, Christopher Gall, in the face. Miraculously, he survived.

From there Baker drove to Bateau bay, about 10 km to the north, where he blasted his own son David, 27, to death. From there Baker drove to nearby North Wyong, where he shot dead Ross Smith, 35, and Smith's girlfriend Leslie Read, 25. Baker claimed Smith owed him money. Leslie Read was a complete stranger.

It would turn out that Baker had broken up with Kerryann Gannan, his de facto wife of seven years, about six weeks earlier, and that he blamed members of her family for the break up.

Two weeks before she was murdered, Kerryann had taken out a restraining order against Baker. Police had confiscated Baker's arsenal of guns but had missed the hidden sawn-off shotgun that would become the mass murder weapon.

At his trial in August 1993, before Justice Newman in the Newcastle Supreme Court, Baker pleaded guilty to six counts of murder and one of attempted murder. It was alleged that Baker told a friend: 'Kerry's father, the bastard, should be shot for the trouble he's caused us. I should go around and shoot the lot of them. Her old man thinks I'm mad. I'll show him how fucking mad I am.'

It was also alleged that Baker had accused his son Dave of sleeping with Kerryann Gannan, and that he (Dave) was giving her drugs. Baker said that 'Dave was going to cop it as well'.

Admitting his guilt, Baker told the court: 'I am very sorry for what's happened in regard to other people's families and being sorry is obviously not enough and never will be.'

The Central Coast Massacre

In sentencing Baker to penal servitude for life, without the possibility of parole, Justice Newman said: 'The total criminality exhibited by the prisoner on the night in question completely overwhelms any subjective matters and accordingly the maximum penalty is called for.

'I have no doubt [that] at the time when he pulled the trigger in relation to the murders (with the exception of Lisa Gannan) and at the time that he shot Mr Gall, the prisoner had but one intent, and that was to kill.'

Outside the court, a distraught Ann Gannan, 40, the mother of the murdered girls, said: 'Just ask any mother what it's like to go stand at a grave and talk to your children. You expect your children to bury you, not you to bury them. That is the most heartbreaking thing any mother could go through ... to have her kid buried.'

'I mean my life's finished, it's finished,' she said. 'There's nothing left. Bring in capital punishment, yes it might stop something. I'm left with no daughters, no grandson, my sons have got no father ... so where's the justice in that?'

Chapter 12

ROBERT ARTHUR SELBY LOWE

The Murder of the Little Girl on the Pink Bike

So shocking was the crime of Robert Arthur Selby Lowe, husband, father, Sunday school teacher and church elder, that as he was sentencing him, on 2 December 1994, Justice Phillip Cummins wiped his eyes as he tried to hold back tears at the horror that had unfolded during Lowe's trial for the murder of a 6-year-old girl.

It was the second time that the kindly judge had been reduced to tears. The first had been during evidence given in the trial when Lowe was alleged to have told a fellow prison inmate that before the child had choked to death or died of sheer fright, or both, as Lowe forced her to do sexual things to him, she had screamed, 'Take me home to mummy. I want my mummy.'

Lowe had been found guilty of the premeditated abduction, sexual assault, murder and concealment of the body of 6-year-old Sheree Beasley, who had disappeared while riding her bike at the Victorian seaside tourist location of Rosebud on 29 June 1991.

It wasn't until almost three months later, in September 1991, that Sheree's decomposed body was

Murder of the Girl on the Pink Bike

found crammed into a stormwater drain almost 15 km from where she had been abducted. It would be revealed at his trial that Lowe had used his feet to cram the dead child further up into the narrow concrete culvert, to avoid detection.

In sentencing Lowe to life in prison and refusing to set a fixed minimum term, and adding that in this case that 'life means life', Justice Cummins slammed the prison doors on the child-murderer forever. Lowe will never be released to molest and kill little girls again.

Justice Cummins then uttered the words that would send a shiver up the spine of every parent: 'What you did was every child's fear ... and every parent's nightmare'.

To all appearances the tall, thin Lowe was a respectable, church-going, hardworking member of the community, happily married with two sons. Lowe was considered an elder of his church, was a Sunday school teacher and gave generously of his time to church community projects.

But the horrible truth was that Lowe had a long list of convictions in England, New Zealand and Australia for stealing, indecent assault on a male, exposing himself to young girls and a variety of other sex offences in public places, and had served two jail terms in New Zealand.

Born in England in January 1937, Lowe was the middle of three boys raised in middle-class Northern English surroundings. In 1956 he was convicted on charges of car theft and injuring a policeman while trying to get away.

In 1959 Lowe moved to New Zealand with his parents and two brothers. Shortly after, he was charged with indecent assault on a male. He moved from Wellington to Auckland, where in 1961 he was sentenced to 6 months jail for sex offences. Back in Wellington in 1964, Lowe was convicted of wilful and obscene exposure and sent back to jail. In 1965 he was convicted of theft.

The Lowe family was prominent in both business and New Zealand society circles, and in 1967, at their instigation, Lowe took a one-way trip to Australia. Here he started work as a salesman, and became a devout Christian.

Through his church, Lowe met deeply-religious Lorraine Sangster, courted her and married her in 1972. Unaware of her husband's past, it wouldn't be until almost two decades later that she would discover the past of the man she had chosen to spend the rest of her life with.

The well mannered, middle-class Lowes kept pretty much to themselves, lived in an average home in the pleasant suburb of Glen Waverley and sent their two boys to private school. Robert Lowe worked diligently as a travelling salesman and he and his wife were devout churchgoers and elders of their church.

On weekends and at vacation time, the Lowe family would go to their holiday flat at the seaside tourist resort of Rosebud, on Port Phillip Bay, just up the road from Portsea, the playground of the well-to-do.

Things were good for the Lowes. Outwardly, at least.

But unknown to his family, Lowe, a habitual liar, had been living a double life as a flasher, exposing himself in public and propositioning young boys and girls. Although he had been apprehended many times for his indiscretions, he had evaded conviction on most occasions by talking himself out of it – convincing the authorities that he was harmless.

In 1984, Lowe received a 12-month good behaviour bond on an obscene exposure charge after he had been caught exposing himself and making sexually suggestive comments to schoolgirls at a shopping centre outside Melbourne.

In 1988 he was arrested in Traralgon, 150 km east of Melbourne, and questioned about a series of offensive conducts, but he was released, and no charges were laid.

In 1990, Lowe was arrested and charged when he approached schoolgirls at Flinders Street railway station while they were waiting for a train and told them that the balloons they were holding looked like 'big dicks' and asked the girls to 'go with him and have sex'. Terrified, the girls ran out onto the street and called a policeman, who tackled Lowe as he fled.

Lowe was charged with obscene behaviour and fined $700. Lowe's psychotherapist, Margaret Hobbs, whom he had been seeing since 1984 and who would eventually play a significant part in bringing him to justice for Sheree Beasley's murder, wrote this damning 'defence' report for Lowe's hearing on the obscenity charges. For obvious reasons, the defence chose not to hand it over to the magistrate – it surely would have put their client back behind bars. In hindsight, this could perhaps have saved Sheree Beasley's life.

Hobbs' report read:

> *I am of the opinion that he (Lowe) truly believes that he is indulging in harmless behaviour ... It does, unfortunately, need the intervention of the courts to instil in him the*

> *illegality of his actions. The censure of the court at this time will assist with any ongoing therapy once it has been clearly demonstrated ... his behaviour is unacceptable to the general community.*

Unfortunately, her patient's past crimes would pale into insignificance next to the enormity of the atrocity that he would soon commit. This crime would see to it that he would take his place among the most evil of killers that Australia has ever known – behind bars forever.

On the cold winter's afternoon of 29 June 1991, Sheree Beasley disappeared while riding her treasured pink bike (and wearing her matching pink bike helmet) to the shops at the Victorian seaside tourist town of Rosebud where she lived with her mother Kerri Greenhill (her maiden name) and her two younger sisters, Crystal and Jacinta.

Sheree had gone to the shops just after 1.00 pm and returned shortly before 2.00 pm, but had to go back as she had forgotten to pick up some of the things she was sent out to get. That was the last time Kerri Greenhill would see her little girl alive.

Police had little to go on except that Sheree's bike was found by the road. It would turn out later that a motorist had found it lying in the middle of the road and had placed it up against a tree so it wouldn't be run over.

Alongside the bike was a shoulder bag containing the items that her mother had asked Sheree to return to the shop to buy. In the following days a 6-year-old boy recalled seeing a small blue car with only two doors pull up and a man get out and pick Sheree up and put her in the front passenger's seat of the car and drive away.

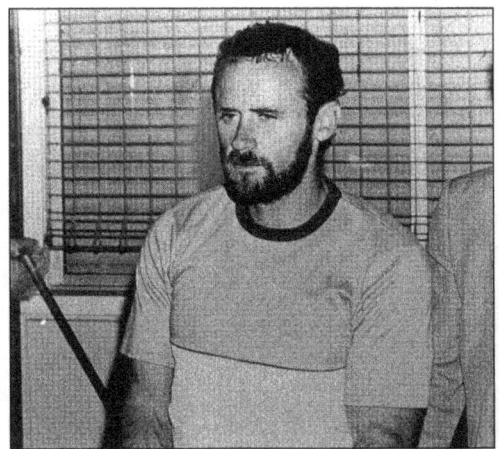

Child killer John David Lewthwaite after his recapture when he escaped from Morisset Psychiatric Hospital in 1975.

(Photo credit News Ltd)

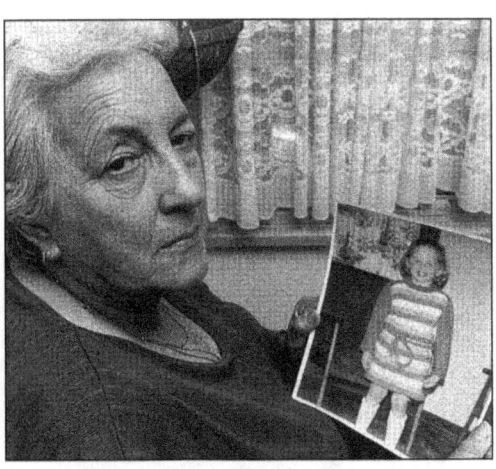

Gwen Hanns with a photo of her 5-year-old daughter, Nicole Margaret Hanns, who John Lewthwaite stabbed to death with a carving knife.

(Photo credit News Ltd)

Never to be Released 2

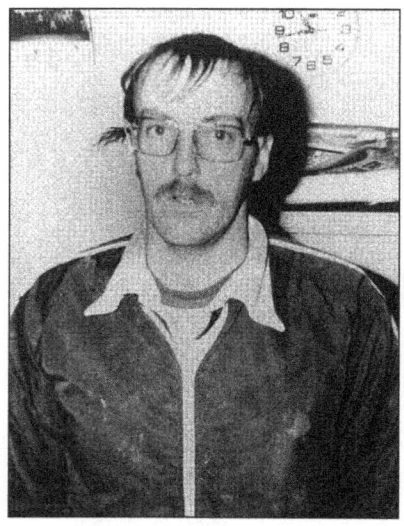

The Griffith Schoolboy Murderer, Michael George Laurance, who sexually assaulted and murdered three boys in the NSW country town of Griffith between 1984 and 1986. Laurance told police that it gave him sexual pleasure watching two of the boys drown in his bathtub.
(Photo credit News Ltd)

The Lonely Hearts Killer, Rodney Francis Cameron, after his arrest for the 1990 serial murder of a woman in a NSW country motel.
(Photo credit News Ltd)

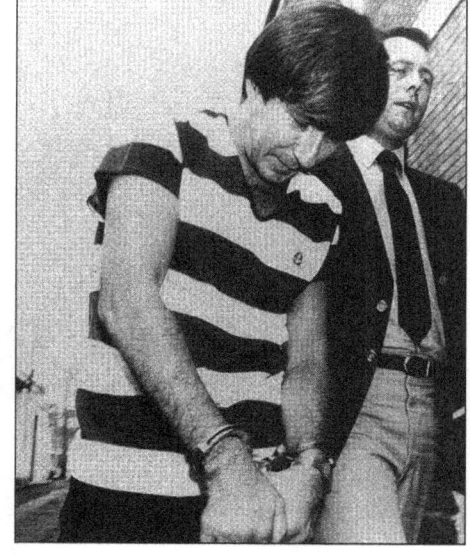

Never to be Released 2

Nine-year-old Ebony Simpson who was sexually assaulted and left to drown by Andrew Peter Garforth in Bargo, NSW in 1992. As a direct result of Ebony's death, her parents, Christine and Peter Simpson, founded the Homicide Victims' Support Group. There are now branches in almost every state throughout Australia.

(Photo Courtesy Christine and Peter Simpson)

Never to be Released 2

Malcolm George Baker killed six innocent people with a shotgun on the night of 28 October, 1992 in what became known as The Central Coast Massacre.

Church elder, husband, father and child killer Robert Arthur Selby Lowe is led away from court after his appeal for the murder of six-year-old Sheree Beasley was dismissed.

(Photo credit Herald and Weekly Times)

Never to be Released 2

Television producer Steve Barrett (left) and 60 Minutes presenter Charles Wooley (right) who featured in the interview with Paul Onions, the man who brought about the undoing of the Backpacker Murderer, Ivan Robert Marko Milat.

Paul Onions, the English backpacker who almost became Ivan Milat's third victim.

Never to be Released 2

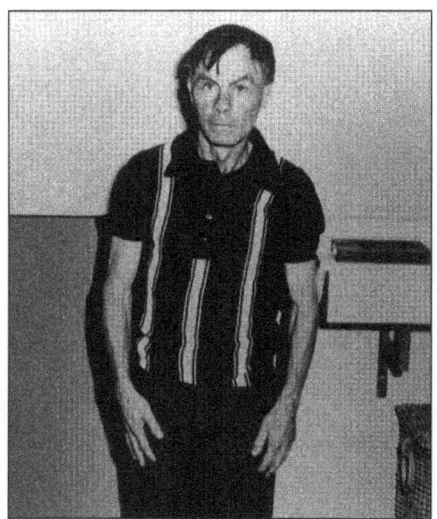

Although no body was ever found, Daryl Francis Suckling was found guilty of the murder of Melbourne prostitute Jodie Maree Larcombe and sentenced to life imprisonment.

Richard William Leonard was sentenced to life, never to be released from prison for the stabbing murder of a Sydney taxi-driver and the bow and arrow murder of a young man who he dismembered and kept in his freezer.
(Photo credit News Ltd)

Never to be Released 2

The St Valentine's Day Murderer, Lindsey Robert Rose confessed to five murders including the stabbing and shooting of two prostitutes on St Valentine's Day. After killing the women, Rose set fire to the brothel where they were working.

Arthur Stanley "Neddy" Smith - crime boss, underworld enforcer, gunman, rapist, heroin dealer, armed robber and multiple-murderer. Smith rose from being a street hoodlum to become Australia's most feared and notorious gangster of modern times.

Arthur Stanley "Neddy" Smith being returned to prison after one of his many court appearances.

Murder of the Girl on the Pink Bike

Another witness told of how she had seen a little girl in a pink bicycle helmet crying her eyes out in the front of a small blue car while it was stopped in traffic about the time of the abduction.

In her statement to police she said, 'I know there were only two people in the car, being the young child and a mature age person. I don't know whether [the adult was] male or female, but they didn't have a beard or moustache. I know the car was very small and I recall it being a hatchback.'

After police showed the witness a variety of small hatchbacks, she positively identified the car she had seen as a Toyota Corolla hatchback. Police then methodically rang every one of the hundreds of Victorian owners of blue Toyota Corolla hatchbacks, asking to talk to the regular drivers or have them call back. One of them was Robert Lowe, who drove a Toyota Corolla hatchback registered to the company he worked for as a sales representative.

Unlike the other drivers who called police back to explain their whereabouts on the day Sheree Beasley went missing, Lowe was abrupt and didn't have to think twice about his alibi, stating that he was at home with his wife and kids. And it had taken him a week to call police back. Lowe also denied that he had any connection with the Rosebud area.

When Lowe refused to give police his home phone number they became suspicious and typed his name into the computer. They were shocked at the result – a long list of charges reading 'offensive behaviour' and 'obscene exposure' appeared.

Police discovered that there was also an ongoing investigation of a man who had exposed himself to

Robert Arthur Selby Lowe

young boys four months earlier at a public swimming pool and fled after being interrupted by school teachers. The teachers took down the number of his blue Toyota Corolla hatchback; it was the same registration as the one Lowe drove.

And, just as it appeared that police may have their first real suspect, Crime Stoppers received an anonymous phone call from a woman telling them of a man who had a history of sex offences and delighted in wilfully exposing himself to children.

The man was currently undergoing therapy for his condition, had a holiday apartment at Rosebud and drove a blue Corolla hatchback. His name was Robert Arthur Selby Lowe.

As police quickly found out, the anonymous woman caller was his psychotherapist, Margaret Hobbs, who had been treating Lowe since 1984 and had suspected for a long time that Lowe had been 'building up' to something sinister.

Undercover police kept Lowe under constant surveillance while they prepared to pay him a visit. Police arrived at the Lowe family home in August 1991 with a search warrant. For the first time in their marriage, Lorraine Lowe was confronted with the truth about her husband's past and, worse still, the possibility that he may be a child-murderer, an allegation which Robert Lowe steadfastly denied.

Lowe was taken away and interviewed at police headquarters and eventually allowed to leave after police couldn't find a reason to hold him. Police also found nothing in his home to link him to Sheree Beasley's abduction.

But the police surveillance continued, and on many

occasions undercover police observed Lowe exposing himself to young girls in public places, picking up prostitutes, hanging around public swimming pools and masturbating in parks and public toilets.

After the raid and a visit by detectives to his workplace, Lowe was fired from his job. His wife ordered him out of the family home and he moved into the apartment at Rosebud.

Lowe's alibi – that he was at home all afternoon on the day of the little girl's disappearance – wasn't holding up either, as his wife and sons told police the truth; they didn't recall seeing him until about 5.00 pm that afternoon.

On 24 September 1993, almost three months after she disappeared, Sheree Beasley's decomposing body was found by two teenagers riding their horses – at Red Hill, some 15 km from where she had been abducted.

Try as they might, police could find nothing to link Lowe to Sheree Beasley's abduction and murder. But they felt sure he was their man.

They found an ally in Margaret Hobbs, whom Lowe was visiting regularly and whom he considered a friend and a confidant.

Over a long period, Hobbs painstakingly managed to get Lowe to admit bits and pieces of what happened on the day of the abduction. Lowe even took Hobbs on a drive to retrace his movements from Rosebud to exactly where Sheree Beasley's body had eventually been found.

What Lowe didn't know was that as he made admission after admission to Hobbs, police were listening in the room next door, and as they drove to the murder and burial scenes, police were not far behind.

In the early hours of 31 March 1993, 21 months after Sheree Beasley had been abducted, police picked up Robert Lowe, who was by now unemployed and homeless, at a backpacker hostel in St Kilda, and charged him with her murder.

And if police hadn't already been 100% convinced that they had a watertight case against Lowe, their fears were laid to rest when they discovered they had a most unexpected collaborator: one of Victoria's most notorious inmates, Peter Allan Reid, a troublesome and extremely violent killer who was doing life for murdering a policeman

Reid had little time for child-murderers, and when Lowe confided in him in Pentridge's K Division, where Lowe was awaiting trial, Reid got word to detectives that he was more than prepared to help them nail Lowe once and for all.

What Peter Reid encouraged Robert Arthur Selby Lowe to confess – how he stalked the little girl, sadistically murdered her and rammed her body into a stormwater drain – will go down in history as one of the most horrifying statements ever produced in a court of law in this country.

Reid's statement was exceptionally long and meticulously detailed and answered all the detectives' questions as to what actually happened on that terrible day in 1991.

The following is an abridged text:

On the 6th of April 1993, another inmate of the prison, Robert Lowe, was transferred to my unit. I became

Murder of the Girl on the Pink Bike

reasonably friendly with Lowe; he seemed to want to talk about why he was there. He told me he was a married man with two children. I knew he had been charged with the murder of Sheree Beasley.

On the 16th of April I decided to start writing things down so that I wouldn't have trouble recalling them when I gave the information to the police. Lowe started telling me he had gone to his house in Rosebud on Saturday the 29th of June 1991, to repair some tiles.

He told me that he started at 11.30 am and finished about thirty minutes later. He said that the neighbours were not around at the time as he had gone to see them as he knew the old man next door had cancer and was very ill. He left his place about 2.00 pm and drove up to an area about seven kilometres away where he saw a little girl riding a pushbike 'all over the place'.

He said he pulled over up the way a bit at a T-intersection or X intersection. He said he got out of his car and waved to the little girl to pull over. He said that she had a blue and pink tracksuit on with a pink and blue helmet.

He said that he told the little girl that her mummy had said for him to take her home as her mummy was ill. He said the little girl became suspicious of him and added that he opened the car door and forced her into the front of his car.

He said he then put a seat belt around her and drove about fifteen kilometres to an inland country area and forced her to do the 'dirty acts'.

He said that from terrifying fear and the act she was forced to do, she choked to death. Lowe would not comment much on the actual 'act'. I don't know why he wouldn't. Lowe further stated that his sperm had gone all over her tracksuit, so he had gotten rid of her clothes. He

Robert Arthur Selby Lowe

said he had taken them off her. He said at that stage she was already dead. He said he went to a sealed road, leaving her in her underwear as he forced her into a stormwater drain.

Lowe told me that on the other side of the road there was a farmhouse set back off the road. He said it had a long low roof and possibly a verandah on the front. From the way he described it, I made a rough sketch of it.

Lowe left her body there and he stated he came back to check it out about three days later, by driving past. He said he didn't stop. Lowe also stated he dumped her clothing into a dumpmaster. He mentioned the name of the street in Blackburn where the bin was, but I couldn't recall what it was at the time.

Lowe told me his car had been taken from him by the police, but that they returned it again four days later. He also stated that on a few occasions the police had interviewed him at the Rosebud police station. Lowe told me from that day on he was being followed.

It was during this period that Lowe stated he went to the public library and checked all the newspapers and media coverage on Sheree Beasley to see if the police had much on him.

Lowe was worried about his wife stuffing up his alibi about being home at 1.00 pm that Saturday the 29th of June 1991, when in fact he was not. He said he collected the little girl about 2.30 to 2.34 pm. I asked him how he remembered this and he said he just knew.

Lowe stated he didn't get home until 4.35 pm that Saturday night, but that he told the cops he got home at 2.00 pm. Lowe stated that his wife had divorced him and that she had taken out a restraining order against him. He told me he wanted her dead, as she was working for the police. He stated

Murder of the Girl on the Pink Bike

she was very sick and he wished she would die. He said that Sheree's mother was in Queensland and that he wanted to get her too. By 'get' her, I believe he meant to kill her. Lowe told me he had $2000 in a bank account and that the bank book or cheque book was being held by his legal advisers. He said he would use this money to have his wife fixed.

On the 18th of April 1993, Lowe asked if I knew anyone who could destroy a typewriter for him as the police would need this typewriter as evidence against him, and that it would be damaging to him if it was found.

He also told me about a lady who was a therapist of some sort and that he needed to make contact with her. He didn't talk much about her and didn't mention her name at any stage. At some later stage he told me this therapist was Margaret Hobbs, who had been my parole officer back in 1981.

On the 21st of April I met with Detective Greg Bowd and Detective O'Neill of the CIB prison liaison squad and told them what had happened and I also handed Bowd a hand-drawn diagram of the scene in relation to Sheree Beasley's death, a handwritten note that Lowe had given me earlier and twelve pages of handwritten notes that I had made in relation to my conversations with Lowe. Sergeant Bowd told me that he would get on to the investigating officers from the homicide squad and they would contact me.

On the 23rd of April I met with Detectives Bowd and Bartsch. I again went over what I'd been told by Lowe with Bartsch, as I wanted to know if he (Bartsch) had been telling the truth or just stringing me along.

I didn't want to go any further with it if Lowe was making a fool of me. I was very angry with Lowe after what he told me about Sheree Beasley's death and I just felt I had to tell someone.

Robert Arthur Selby Lowe

Later that day I had a conversation with Lowe in relation to Sheree Beasley's death. I recorded this conversation in note form after we had been separated. He also said he had taken his own clothes off when he got home later that afternoon. He said he washed his clothes the same day as they had dirt all over them and there were other stains on them.

He told me he removed mats from the front of the car and scrubbed them. He also told me he took some blood-stained paper out of the car, but couldn't tell me anything about it, or whose blood it was. He told me he cleaned all of the inside of the car with detergent.

He then told me he hosed the outside of the car down, cleaning everything, including the wheels and the underside. After that he said he drove the car off the driveway and hosed down the driveway as well. He added that he paid special attention to the seats in his car.

Lowe then told me he did not bother to take Sheree's helmet off until later on in the car. He was unsure, but said he could have taken it off on the way to Chinaman's Creek.

Lowe said the reason he went all the way out to where he did was that he knew the area well and didn't want to run the risk of going back into an open freeway. He said he went to a bushy area off a sealed road and parked the car on a dirt road. He then went on to the area where he decided to bury her.

Lowe also told me that he now recalled the foreshore area where he picked up Sheree Beasley, stating it was an unsealed road. Lowe went on to tell me that at the time he picked Sheree Beasley up, he admonished a 10-year-old boy for picking on her. Lowe told me that after he picked up the girl, he left her bike on the road or just off to the side of it. He told me he lifted the girl straight off the bike. Again I decided to get him to make a hand-sketched plan of the area.

Murder of the Girl on the Pink Bike

He went on to tell me that he had seen the girl, Sheree, at the shops in the past, but when I pressed him as to when that might have been, he couldn't remember. He told me the only person he had told about Sheree was Margaret (Hobbs). He said he hadn't told her as much about the case as he had told me.

Lowe went on to say that at the time of Sheree's death, he didn't have a beard and that the reason he had one now was to confuse witnesses and identification. Lowe stated he wore glasses when kidnapping Sheree, as he couldn't drive without them.

On the 24th of April I again had further discussions with Lowe. As a starting point I asked him how dirty his car was and he said he remembered getting his car bogged at some stage when he was on the unsealed road. He drew a rough map of the area.

Lowe stated [that] he did not go down to Rosebud on the day of Sheree's abduction purely to fix the tiles in his flat. He said he just used the tile-fixing story as an excuse to justify being away from his wife. Lowe had made a comment that he had been watching the little girl for some time and that she had been at the shops before.

I asked him how many times he had seen her in the past and he said numerous times. I asked Lowe whether the rest of the family came home before or after him on the day of Sheree Beasley's abduction. Lowe told me one of his sons got back from a friend's place about 5.00 pm that day ... Lowe further stated that he burnt some rags and paper material in his barbeque area and then scattered the ashes over the lawn. He believed his wife may have witnessed this.

On the 25th of April, I got Lowe to draw maps and asked him to notate, in his own handwriting, the various points of interest. I then questioned Lowe further about cleaning his car and he made a comment about having difficulty cleaning a bloodstain on the front passenger side seat, where he had seated Sheree Beasley.

He told me he had first vacuumed the car on Sunday the 30th of June, the day after the abduction. He said he did his wife's car at the same time. He said he used a chamois to clean blood off the edge of the front seat and he also used a detergent to clean it. I asked him where the blood came from and he said, 'the little girl vomited it up when she was choking'.

I asked Lowe if he had been to Rosebud prior to the Saturday of the abduction and he told me he had gone to Rosebud the weekend before, to drop off a fridge at the unit.

It was on this trip that he first noticed the little girl walking along the roadside with her bike. He said she was walking towards Melbourne to the shop Lowe had earlier told me about. Lowe told me he decided on the following Monday to go back to Rosebud and drive around for a while.

He said he again saw the girl on the Monday afternoon there in Rosebud and that she was walking her bike. Lowe told me he followed her from the shop, back to her house, just down from the shop. The following Saturday, Lowe told me he went to Rosebud, not first and foremost to fix the tiles. Again, he said he just used that as an excuse.

Lowe went on to tell me that he spent very little time at the flat that Saturday. He said he vacated the Rosebud unit about 12.30 pm and waited for the little girl to come to the shop. Lowe said he made his move when the little girl and the boy she was with were on their way back from the shop.

Lowe stated he said something to the boy at the time, similar to 'Don't get upset. Don't fight'. Lowe stated he did drive into a short unsealed road at the time. He then marked this on the map.

Murder of the Girl on the Pink Bike

Lowe told me he decided to take the girl's helmet off when she was choking. He also told me he had been watching the girl's house and drew it on the map for me. He also made a couple of comments that sickened me. He stated, 'They say the little girl would have been submissive as her mother was a prostitute.'

He also told me that before the little girl choked, she screamed, 'Take me home to mummy. I want my mummy.'

On the 26th of April I handed Detectives Bowd and Bartsch seven pages of notes I had made over the previous couple of days, as well as Lowe's hand-drawn map of his movements on the day of the abduction, starting at the spot he took Sheree [to and] up to the place her body was found.

On the 29th of April Lowe drew maps of the scene where Sheree Beasley's body was found. He also drew up a list of 'problems' and 'worries and concerns'. I believe all of this was captured on the security videos in K Division.

On the 30th of April Detective Bartsch fixed a tape recorder to my body so that I could tape my conversations with Lowe. At the end of those conversations, I returned to my cell, took the tape recorder off and placed it in a box in my bed for safe keeping. I told Prison Officer Johnson about this and he agreed to take the tape and give it to the police.

Lowe also signed a drawing of the place where Sheree Beasley's body was found at Red Hill. I had drawn this map using Lowe's description of the scene. Lowe acknowledged it as being accurate and correct. I kept the drawing in my cell for safe keeping.

On the 1st of May I again discussed the Sheree Beasley case with Lowe. Lowe gave me a copy of a letter he was sending to Channel 7, asking them to clarify their programming on the 30th of June 1991. I think he meant the 29th of June, the day of Sheree Beasley's abduction. He said he needed this information so he could prepare a believable alibi statement.

Lowe also asked me if I could arrange for someone to get rid of a ticket for a mini-golf place in Rosebud. Apparently he was scared it would prove he had been to the same shop as the little girl and that it would also prove he had been to the shop next door, where he used the ticket. Lowe stated he was also concerned the shop owner might identify him as having been in the same shop where the little girl did her shopping.

On the 2nd of May, Lowe told me about his background and his thoughts and I lost my temper, calling him a dirty old man. He agreed with me, saying that he was sick.

Lowe went on to write out extensive notes about the Beasley case. There were eight pages in all. In these notes he outlined, in chronological order, the events of the investigation into the death of Sheree Beasley and how he was involved in the investigation.

He went on to outline certain things about her death that he guessed and how he had come to write about certain things about his past. He signed the bottom of each page and gave his permission for me to use these pages as he wanted my advice about the preparation of his defence.

I kept all of the notes and sketches he gave me and handed them over to Detective Bartsch about 1 pm on the 3rd of May, along with the drawing of the scene at Red Hill and the black and white copies of Melway maps showing the route he took on the 29th of June 1991.

On the 5th of May, Lowe and I discussed the possibility of Sheree Beasley's missing helmet being found and what it would mean to Lowe. Lowe wrote me out a short letter about how his fingerprints may have come to be on the bike

Murder of the Girl on the Pink Bike

helmet. He said he had been warned by police in Rosebud not to ride his bicycle without a helmet, so he went to K-Mart and picked up a number of helmets to see if he could buy one. He said that if a helmet turned up later with his prints on it then he could fall back on this excuse as to why they were there.

I spoke to Lowe about the Sheree Beasley matter and at the end of the conversation I returned to my cell where I took the recorder, placed it in my drawing instrument box and left it in my bed for safe keeping. Prison Officer Johnson picked up the tape later that day.

I had a day away from Lowe after this and then continued asking him things about Sheree Beasley. Lowe told me that he had made many mistakes in this case and said he would 'use Valium on little girls next time'.

Lowe mentioned that Margaret Hobbs pressured him into going to the site at Red Hill. He had agreed that he had Margaret take him to the site at Red Hill so he could justify having been there purely because of Hobbs.

Lowe also told me he had gotten rid of some underwear and some porno books in a dumpmaster in Glen Waverley. He said he didn't want his wife seeing them, yet he added he'd had them for years. Lowe also claimed Margaret Hobbs told him to put in his confession that he put Sheree Beasley's helmet and clothing in the dumpmaster at Glen Waverley.

I spoke to Lowe about his 'alibi'. He told me he'd say a Chinese fellow helped him to build a fence on the 29th of June 1991. He also told me he dug a hole and planted an apple tree. He said his son came in via a back gate after 5 pm. He said the reason his son never saw him was because he'd concealed himself behind the tool shed while he was working.

Robert Arthur Selby Lowe

Lowe told me that if the neighbours said he wasn't at home on the day, he would say he went up to McEwans to get some nails so he could help the Chinese fellow fix or build his fence.

On the 13th of May, Lowe marked a map with a circle and a cross. These marks show where he reckons he buried Sheree Beasley's helmet. Lowe again began talking about what he had done on the 29th of June 1991, and how he had abducted Sheree Beasley. He also went on to tell me about what happened after that and how he put her body in the drain at Red Hill.

At the end of Lowe telling me about all of these things, I returned to my cell where I took the tape recorder from my body and placed it in a box that I had previously put my drawing instruments in. I put it in my bed so the Prison Officer Johnson could collect it for the police.

After this, Lowe became suspicious of me as he was worried about what happened to his drawings and as to why I asked him to keep repeating things. He began to trust me less and less, and in time, we hardly spoke at all. He actually accused me of working for the police at one stage and I shouted at him, putting on an act that I was really upset by his allegations.

On the 11th of June, Lowe received a copy of the brief of evidence against him. He showed me the brief and let me listen to copies of tapes of conversations between him and Margaret Hobbs. He let me do this as I felt he wanted my help and he wanted to stay on my good side.

On the 16th of June, the relationship between Lowe and I had deteriorated to such a point that Prison Officer Sneddon moved Lowe to another part of the unit. I have kept apart from Robert Lowe since this date. I have not spoken to him since.

Murder of the Girl on the Pink Bike

It took the jury just five hours to reach their guilty verdict. The courtroom erupted in cheers as the cold-blooded child-killer, the remorseless Robert Arthur Selby Lowe, was taken back to prison.

Lowe's sentencing two days later was an extremely emotional affair, and Justice Cummins didn't hold back in his contempt for the prisoner. He said that he accepted Peter Reid's evidence that Sheree Beasley choked to death while forced to perform oral sex on Robert Lowe.

Justice Cummins made note that the evidence revealed in court showed that the egocentric Lowe had no emotion for the little girl and obviously enjoyed reliving the events surrounding her horrible death.

After sentencing Lowe to life in prison with no possibility of parole, Justice Cummins added, 'You have shown yourself, Mr Lowe, to be very intelligent, very articulate and very manipulative in your dealings with the police.'

Robert Arthur Selby Lowe may well ponder these words as he serves out his sentence.

In an ironic twist of fate, the woman who played a major part in bringing Lowe to justice, the psychotherapist Margaret Hobbs, was killed in a car accident in January 1996.

Sheree Beasley's pink bicycle helmet was never found.

Chapter 13

IVAN ROBERT MARKO MILAT

The Backpacker Murders

Englishman Paul Onions is the only person to have stared down the barrel of Ivan Milat's gun and lived. And just as well, because if he hadn't, Ivan Milat could still be a free man and still killing.

As it is, Milat shares the dubious honour of being the most prolific serial killer in Australia's history with Truro murderers James Miller and the late Christopher Worrell.

In all, Ivan Robert Marko Milat murdered seven young backpackers in the Belanglo State Forest south of Sydney between 1989 and 1992. And there seems little doubt that if it were not for Paul Onions, Milat would have killed many more.

And tragically, if rural police had acted a lot more efficiently on Onion's report of the 1990 incident with Ivan Milat, the killer could possibly have been apprehended a lot sooner. Had he been convicted then of attempted murder, he would have been given a stiff sentence due to his extensive past record. This would have saved the lives of the later victims.

The first indication that there was a madman on the loose (except for Onion's report of the incident, which was temporarily lost) in the picturesque NSW southern

The Backpacker Murders

highlands, was the discovery of the remains of two British female backpackers in the Belanglo State Forest on 19 September 1992.

The girls, Caroline Clark and Joanne Walters, both 22, had been reported missing five months earlier on 18 April 1992, during the Easter break. They were found not far from where Paul Onions made his lucky escape from Ivan Milat.

When he read in the English papers back home of the finding of the two English girls' remains, and saw a map showing where the bodies had been discovered – the same area where he had almost been killed by Milat – it confirmed to Paul Onions what he had suspected for a long time; what had happened to him was not a robbery at all, but part of something much more sinister.

But having reported the incident to the police already, he figured that if what happened to him was relevant, they would get in touch with him. No one did.

His suspicions were further confirmed almost a year later when the remains of another five young hitchhikers, three women and two men, were found in the same area. All had been ritualistically murdered, and there were indications that they had all been sexually assaulted. And police made no bones about the fact that they thought that there was more than one murderer involved.

As soon as he read of the finding of the remains of the five other backpackers, Paul Onions rang Australian police, who unearthed his report of the incident with Milat and eventually flew him out him to Australia. He identified Milat from photographs and then returned to give critical evidence at Milat's trial.

Ivan Robert Marko Milat

After Milat's trial and conviction, Australian *60 Minutes* reporter Charles Wooley and producer Steve Barrett flew to England for an exclusive interview with Paul Onions about exactly what happened on that fateful day – 25 January 1990 – the day that would become the undoing of the serial killer who, only three weeks earlier, had murdered his first two victims and concealed their bodies in the dense Belanglo State Forest.

It looks very much as if Paul Onions, 24, the ex-British Navy sailor and Birmingham airconditioning mechanic who had left his job to hitchhike around Australia, was to have been Ivan Milat's next victim.

Here is the edited text of the very long preliminary interview with *60 Minutes* producer Steve Barrett:

I called in at the shop for a can of Coke and as I came out this man asked me if I wanted a lift. He had a big moustache, like the cricketer Dennis Lillee, and was driving a silver 4WD. I couldn't believe my good luck.

He said his name was Bill and asked me where I was travelling and I said I was going towards Canberra and I was trying to get to Mildura, but he asked would Canberra do as he was heading that way. It sounded great.

After about an hour and a half, after we had passed through the township of Mittagong, his speech became aggressive, and instead of being a friendly kind of guy, he changed all of a sudden. He started checking me out and asking what I'd done for work and things like that.

And then he started complaining about all the people who live in Australia and saying things like there's too many immigrants in this country and going on about the Asians. Although I found it a bit odd, I just agreed with him. I felt a little bit uneasy.

The Backpacker Murders

Then he started slowing down a little bit and looking in the rear vision mirrors. He explained that he lost radio reception this far out of town and he wanted to play some tapes that were under the driver's seat. I found this a bit odd because there were tapes on the seat between us.

Then he pulled over to the side of the road and got out and started messing round with the seat. I was a bit nervous and I thought I'd just get out and stretch my legs and try to suss things out.

He became aggressive and asked me what I was getting out for and I said I was stretching my legs. So I was pacing up and down that side of the vehicle as the cars went whizzing past.

He was messing about under the seat and I couldn't really see what he was doing. I found it a bit nervy. I got back in. He watched me as I put the seatbelt back on. He was still messing about under the seat.

Once he saw me get back in, he got back in but then got back out again, telling me that he still hadn't found the tapes. He started fossicking around under the seat again. I thought, 'Oh God, there's something wrong now, what's going to happen next?'

Then I was looking down the barrel of this big black revolver with the copper heads of the bullets showing in the chambers and he was telling me that I was being robbed. I undid my seat belt and he started demanding that I put it back on. I remember telling him to calm down, saying 'What's up, what's up?' as he pointed the gun aggressively at me and told me to calm down because my voice was trembling.

Next thing he had produced a coil of rope and when I saw it I thought, that's it, I'm getting out of here. With that I undid my seatbelt, opened the door, jumped out and ran up the road for my life against the traffic on the highway.

Ivan Robert Marko Milat

I heard him shout 'Stop, get back in here, stop or I'll shoot you'. Then I heard the gun go off but I never looked back. I thought 'Oh God, I've really got to try and make a car stop now'.

But no one would stop. Instead they swerved to miss me and kept going as I frantically tried to wave them down with him running after me. He caught up with me and grabbed me by the shirt and ripped it. He was standing right beside me and staring at me. He was a lot taller and bigger than me. We were standing in the middle of the road.

We were about 50 metres from his vehicle and he was telling me to get back in the car.

He looked round and realised that nobody was stopping for me and kept on insisting that I get back in the car.

I quickly weighed up the situation and I decided that no matter what, I was going to stop the next vehicle that comes along even if it runs over me. I thought that if I was going to die, I'd rather get killed by a car.

I looked at this guy and I thought if I go back there, to me it seemed like it was the end, so I looked the other way and I thought I don't care what happens to the next vehicle, I'm just going to jump in front of it and make it stop. That was the decision I made in about a second.

I turned round and faced the traffic and when the next vehicle, a family van, came across over the rise I put both my hands out in front for it to stop. And as soon as it did I pulled around to the side and opened the sliding door on the passenger side and got in and locked it. There were two women and five children inside and they were all yelling at me to get out and I was saying 'He's got a gun, he's got a gun'.

The lady driver conferred with the lady next to her and obviously made a hasty decision to help me. Ivan Milat was making his way back to the car but was still watching what

The Backpacker Murders

was going on. The lady then put the van in reverse and drove away from the scene in reverse.

She turned the vehicle back onto the other side of the road by bouncing across the wide grassy medium strip and headed back in the opposite direction on the other side of the freeway.

Then I turned around and looked back, just as he turned and he was just standing there with this strange funny grin on his face. I will never forget it as long as I live.

The lady who stopped for me was Mrs Joanne Berry, who was with her sister Gai and their five kids. They were heading home to Canberra. She was kind enough to drive me to the nearest police station at Bowral after we found that the Berrima Police Station was shut. She was almost as frantic as I was, as she didn't really know what was happening except that someone had a gun and she could see the state I was in.

Joanne took me into the Bowral Police Station and told the female constable on duty that I had just been shot at. The constable, Janet Nicholson, gave me a cup of tea to calm me down and took all of the details.

She could just see the state I was in and Joanne was explaining the scene she'd just come across as she was driving down the Hume Highway. She was a bit nervy herself.

The police didn't take me back to where it happened, they just took a detailed report of the incident and put the description of the 4WD out over the air and told them that the driver was wanted in connection with firearm offences relating to the incident.

A senior police officer took me into a quiet room and showed me a bunch of pictures of people who were missing and told me that I was lucky and practically gave me a lecture on the dangers of hitchhiking.

Ivan Robert Marko Milat

They took a statement from Joanne, who didn't really get a look at Milat, and told her she could go. They gave me $20 because I had lost my rucksack containing my camera, clothing, an air ticket and my passport. They then pointed me in the direction of the railway station and I walked down to catch the train back to Sydney.

I can tell you I was very jittery walking down to the railway station, and I probably sat there for about an hour waiting for the train. I still thought he might pop out from anywhere. I made sure I sat near people on the train.

From the police station I had phoned my friend at the Hereford Lodge in Glebe, Sydney, and booked a room for the night. I got a new passport through the British Embassy and took a job in Sydney and waited for my girlfriend to come out from England to join me for the rest of my holiday.

She arrived in May and we saw the east coast of Australia by public transport. We left Australia to return home on 21 June and never heard another word about the incident.

About two years later, in September 1992, I was reading about the discovery of the remains of the two English girls who had gone missing at Easter the same year and the map showed that they had been found in the Belanglo State Forest near Bowral.

It was then that I realised that my incident could have been related. But then I thought no, it can't be, it's too coincidental, so I didn't contact anybody then. And I thought at the time that I'd already given my report and I was pretty sure if it had anything to do with me they'd contact me. (At this stage Paul Onions had no idea that his report had been lost in paperwork and the incident all but forgotten.)

It wasn't until about a year later, when the remains of the other five bodies were discovered in the same area, that I

The Backpacker Murders

thought it seemed strange that no one had contacted me about the man who tried to kill me.

It got big coverage in England and the papers said that they were looking for a serial killer. Then a friend called me from Australia and suggested that I should ring the hotline number and tell them again what happened.

So I went to my local police station in England and I sat down with the detective there and went through it all over again and he suggested I phone the Australian Embassy who put me in touch with the Task Force and I spoke to a detective there and told him the whole story, of which he had no knowledge.

A few months later a detective from the Task Force contacted me. I told him the whole story all over again and within two weeks I was on a plane back to Australia.

They unearthed my report and took me down to the scene where it happened and I described the man with the droopy black mustache who called himself 'Bill' who had fired at me. I gave them a statement and came back to England.

Then the next thing, I don't know how many months later, I got a phone call from the Task Force telling me that somebody was going to be arrested the following day.

The next thing I know is that a man had been arrested in connection with the murders and the attempted murder on me.

The escape of Paul Onions must have shaken Ivan Milat, as he seems to have stopped killing for almost a year. His next victim was solo German backpacker Simone Schmidl, who disappeared while hitchhiking on the Hume Highway near the Belanglo State Forest on 20 January 1991.

Ivan Robert Marko Milat

Then German backpacking couple Gabor Neugebauer and Anja Habschied disappeared while hitchhiking on the Hume Highway on 26 December 1991.

And on 18 April 1992, Joanne Walters and Caroline Clark, the English backpackers, went missing while hitchhiking south along the Hume Highway.

And Milat had already murdered Australian couple Deborah Everist and her boyfriend James Gibson on 30 December 1989, just three weeks before he tried to abduct Paul Onions.

After the bodies of Simone Schmidl, Gabor Neugebauer, Anja Habschied, Deborah Everist and James Gibson were found in October and November 1993, after a massive police search, police made up a list of possible offenders with similar previous offences. Ivan Milat's name was on that list – his criminal record was extensive – but police had no reason to suspect that he was the serial killer.

Since he had committed his first offence in 1962 as a 17-year-old, Milat had been in prison four times for an assortment of stealing offences, and had been charged with the rape of a woman in 1971 and with armed robbery.

Secretly flown in from England on 2 May, Paul Onions didn't have the slightest hesitation in identifying Ivan Milat from photographs and he became suspect number one. From then on his every move was watched by police.

They would find out that Milat used to drive a silver Nissan 4WD and he was on days off from his job as a road worker every time a murder was committed. It was all starting to come together.

The Backpacker Murders

It would have taken a lot longer, or perhaps the murders would not have been solved at all, without the eyewitness account Paul Onions.

At 6.40 am on the morning of 22 May 1994, a convoy of vehicles full of armed police descended on Ivan Milat's home in Eagle Vale in Sydney's southwest and arrested him. He was charged with the murders of seven backpackers and the attempted murder of another.

At Ivan Milat's home police found articles of clothing and items that were positively identified as belonging to the victims. Gear also belonging to the victims and Paul Onions was found at the homes of Milat's brothers, Richard and Walter, and at his mother's home.

Ivan Milat pleaded not guilty to murder. At the trial it was revealed that the seven young backpackers had been sexually assaulted, stabbed, shot, used as target practice, decapitated, tortured, hacked and bludgeoned to death.

The horrors that detectives found in Ivan Milat's killing fields were so unspeakably cruel and sadistic that police wondered if they were dealing with just the one murderer.

So did the defence, which implied that Ivan Milat's brother Richard could quite easily have carried out the attack on Paul Onions and that Ivan had been mistakenly identified.

The defence also said that 'it was absolutely irrefutable that whoever has committed these offences must be either within the Milat family or so very closely associated with it, it doesn't much matter. Blind Freddy can see that. There can be absolutely no doubt.

Ivan Robert Marko Milat

The question is, who is it within the Milat family who has committed these eight offences?'

No charges have been laid against any other member of the Milat family in relation to the murders.

After three days of deliberation, the jury returned a guilty verdict on seven counts of murder and one of the attempted murder of Paul Onions.

In his summing up, Justice David Hunt said: 'It is sufficient here to record that each of the victims was attacked savagely and cruelly, with force which was unusual and vastly more than was necessary to cause death, and for some form of psychological gratification. Each of two of the victims was shot a number of times in the head. A third was decapitated in circumstances which establish that she would have been alive at the time. The stab wounds to each of the other three would have caused paralysis, two of them having had their spinal cords completely severed. The multiple stab wounds to three of the seven victims would have been likely to have penetrated their hearts. There are signs that two of them were strangled. All but one appears to have been sexually interfered with before or after death.'

Ivan Robert Marko Milat was jailed for the term of his natural life on seven counts of murder and to 6 years for the attempted abduction of Paul Onions.

We can only wonder what would have happened had Ivan Milat been arrested, charged and sent to prison when he attempted to abduct Paul Onions. Would Milat have been implicated in the murders of the Australian couple he had killed three weeks earlier when their bodies turned up three years later? We shall never know.

And of the $500,000 reward that Paul Onions is eligible to claim but still hasn't? 'The reward is that I've got my life,' he told reporter Charles Wooley. 'I'm happy with that, really. Anything else is a bonus.'

Chapter 14

EDWIN STREET

The Bodies in the Shopping Bags

Bushranger Ned Kelly and Edwin Street, 42-year-old wife-killer, had little in common except that they both said 'such is life' in the face of a horrible fate.

These were the last words Kelly uttered before he was hanged, and they were the last words spoken by Street as he was led from the court to spend the rest of his life behind bars, 'never to be released', for the murders of two Sydney women.

Street's de facto wife Dawn, 42, a charity worker who cared for quadriplegics, was found buried in a large shopping bag in a Sydney park on 17 December 1993. Edwin Street claimed that he last saw her when she left their home to buy some milk at 8.30 pm on 29 November.

After the discovery of her body, Street made an emotional appeal to the general public for help to solve the crime. Street said in his plea: 'Anyone with any information should let somebody know, because if I have to come out and do my own little investigation, I will.'

On 23 February 1994, police investigating the murder found the body of another woman in a bag at Street's home in Enmore, in Sydney's inner west.

The Bodies in the Shopping Bags

In his statement to police, Street said that he had snapped when his wife told him one of her ex-boyfriends was a better lover than he was. Street said he held a pillow over his wife's face, then had a few drinks and went to sleep. When he awoke the following morning, his wife was dead.

Street told police that he put the body in a bag and then in a suitcase and caught a cab to Berrys Island Reserve at Wollstonecraft, a northern Sydney suburb, where he buried it.

When the body was discovered, it was in an advanced state of decomposition, and no definite cause of death could be established, though the post mortem revealed that there were signs of suffocation.

Police had gone to Street's home in February 1994 to collect some of his wife's clothes to assist them in their investigations. When they asked Street for a suitcase to put the clothes in, and opened another bag, they found the body of Linda Whitton, who had been living with Street for less than a week. She had known him only for a short time.

Street said that Linda Whitton had stabbed herself seven times before he could get the knife from her. One of the stab wounds was in her back.

Street was found guilty of the murders at his trial at the Supreme Court before Justice Dunford, who said Street's story about Linda Whitton stabbing herself was 'obviously absurd, as the jury has found' and described the murders of the two women, who were both small and both epileptic, as brutal. 'I regard the prospects of rehabilitation as only slight, and the risks of his re-offending as significant.'

At Street's sentencing on 29 June 1995, Justice

Edwin Street

Dunford said Street had a 'terrifying record of physical violence, particularly toward women'. Street had a number of convictions for carnal knowledge and indecent assault, and in 1989 was sentenced to 4 years' jail for attacking a young woman who rejected his sexual advances.

'The maximum penalty is intended for the worst category of cases, [and] I regard the quite separate murders of two women some 12 weeks apart as amongst the worst category of cases,' Justice Dunford said.

The judge then imposed the maximum sentence available under the truth-in-sentencing legislation: life without hope of parole. As he was led from the court, Street uttered Ned Kelly's immortal words – 'such is life'.

Chapter 15

MARTIN BRYANT

The Port Arthur Massacre

Author's note.
I feel so strongly about what this man did on that horrible Sunday of 28 April 1996 that it troubles me writing about it. Besides, I believe that enough words have already been written about the horrors that occurred on this blackest of black days in our history and about the man who carried them out.

And while I am aware of and deeply respectful of the wishes of the families and loved ones of the victims, who wish that the memories of the deceased be kept alive forever, I have no intention of saying anything more about these shocking murders and how they happened than has to be said.

In fact, if there were some way that I could leave this chapter out of the book, I would, not out of disrespect for the deceased, but so as not to give the killer any more notoriety than he has already, as notoriety is about all he has left in his life (and to my mind he shouldn't even have that).

But the killer was sentenced 'never to be released', and that is what this book is about, so he is entitled to a place here, which I have begrudgingly given him.

Martin Bryant

I am not going to refer to him by name in this edited chronology of what happened. He will be referred to simply as "the Killer".

The Killer is in good company in Tasmania's only maximum security prison, Risdon. Risdon is situated about 10 km from Tasmania's capital, Hobart. It is a small jail, and houses Tasmania's worst 200 offenders.

The Killer's co-inhabitants include Richard Dickinson, who kicked his mother to death because she complained that he was playing the stereo too loudly, Aaron Jeffrey, who was picked up by police while goading a couple of gorillas into a fight in the Melbourne Zoo after he had killed his father in Tasmania and fled to the mainland, and the infamous Dr Rory Jack Thompson, aka Jack Newman, the oceanographer who chopped his wife up into manageable parts and flushed her down the toilet.

One of Risdon's most celebrated inmates, author, humorist and self-confessed mass murderer, Mark Chopper Read, was released in February 1998.

Obviously, only Tasmania's worst offenders are sent to Risdon. And for what he did, the Killer will spend the rest of his life there.

Journalists who have been to Risdon with hopes of talking with the Killer or at least getting some pictures of him in his surroundings have come away sadly disappointed.

Journalists are not allowed to take pictures of him or interview him. The few that have been allowed inside the prison to view the Killer's living conditions have not been allowed to carry cameras or tape recorders within view of the Killer.

Reports indicate that the Killer used to inquire

The Port Arthur Massacre

regularly as to how he was being depicted by the media and how history would remember him.

He will be remembered as the most cold-blooded killer in modern times.

Shortly after 1.00 pm on Sunday, 28 April 1996, the Killer entered the Broad Arrow café at Port Arthur, the old convict settlement on Tasmania's southern peninsula.

He was carrying a large tennis bag, and after he had eaten a hasty meal he took a semi-automatic rifle from the bag and opened fire on the lunchtime diners, picking them off one at a time rather than taking pot luck by simply spraying the dining room with bullets.

The Killer left the carnage in the café and walked outside, killing at random as he went. He approached a car, shot the lady driver and ordered the man out at gunpoint. He then forced the man to get into the boot of a BMW and took off, leaving 32 dead men, women and children behind him.

From Port Arthur the Killer drove to the Seascape guest house 2.5 km away, where he killed the husband-and-wife owners and the man he had put in the boot of the car. After an all-night siege with police, during which many shots were fired, the Killer set fire to the guest house and was eventually arrested shortly after 8.00 am as he ran from the building with his clothes on fire.

On 22 November 1996, Tasmania's Chief Justice William Cox sentenced the Killer to jail for the term of his natural life on 35 counts of murder, 20 counts of attempted murder, three of causing grievous bodily harm, eight of wounding, four of aggravated assault, one of arson and one of unlawfully setting fire to property.

The youngest victim was three, the oldest seventy-two.

As the Killer was taken from the courtroom to spend the rest of his life behind bars, someone in the crowd called out; 'May you rot in hell.'

Chapter 16

DARYL FRANCIS SUCKLING

The Mysterious Death of Jodie Larcombe

On or around about 22 December 1987, the day she was released from Pentridge prison, 22-year-old prostitute and heroin addict Jodie Maree Larcombe went missing.

In March 1988, in an unrelated incident, police were called to an isolated property in Pooncarie, in the southwest of NSW, to investigate the sexual assault and abduction of a woman named Sophie Carni, who had miraculously escaped from her assailant.

They arrested 53-year-old Daryl Francis Suckling, a property caretaker, and charged him with sexual assault and wrongful imprisonment. Suckling had an extensive criminal history – 138 convictions for various offences, including sexual assault, dating back to when he was 11 years old.

Sophie Carni told police that her assailant had abducted her at knifepoint in Melbourne, taken her to the property in NSW, raped her and forced her to pose for pornographic photos.

In her statement, she also mentioned that her assailant had told her that he had killed another woman and that the woman's body was buried in a property nearby. But he didn't say exactly where. Police conducted a thorough search of the farm and surrounding areas but no body was ever found.

But while they found no human remains in their search, police did find jewellery, clothing and a set of dentures that belonged to Jodie Larcombe, who had gone missing three months earlier.

But it was the discovery of pornographic photos of Jodie Larcombe, who appeared to be drugged or drunk, and whose body appeared to be battered and bruised, that led police to believe that she was the woman Suckling had boasted of killing and burying.

On 3 April 1989, police charged Daryl Suckling with the murder of Jodie Larcombe and with charges against Sophie Carni. Trial dates were set for 1990.

On 3 June 1989, Sophie Carni died of a drug overdose. Her evidence was now inadmissible, and the judge ordered that Suckling be acquitted of charges in relation to her.

But Suckling still had the charges of abducting and murdering Jodie Larcombe to answer, and his trial date was set down for 25 February 1991.

Soon after, police prosecutors and Jodie Larcombe's family were shocked to receive a letter from the NSW Director of Public Prosecutions (DPP), Reg Blanch, informing them that the trial of Daryl Suckling on the charge of murdering Jodie Larcombe would not go ahead.

The letter from Mr Blanch said, in part: 'I advise you that after careful consideration of this matter, I have directed that there be no further prosecution. I have received advice from two Queen's Counsel that the evidence available at this time is such that if the

Mysterious Death of Jodie Larcombe

evidence which is admissible were presented to a jury, a verdict of acquittal would be inevitable.

'I agree with the assessment. Such an acquittal would make it impossible to prosecute the matter again. By directing now that there be no further proceedings, it is open to prosecute the matter again if any relevant evidence should come forward.'

Mr Blanch and the NSW Department of Public Prosecutions came under heavy fire for the decision and in February 1992, Mr Blanch explained why he had made the decision not to go ahead with the Suckling case.

These were the facts of the case.

No one had seen or heard of Jodie Larcombe since she was released from Pentridge on 22 December 1987. She lived and worked in St Kilda. On 26 December 1987, Daryl Suckling drew $40 from an automatic teller machine in that suburb. This was the amount that Jodie Larcombe charged for oral sex.

In March 1988, police found Jodie Larcombe's false teeth, silver chain and watch in Suckling's possession at his remote Wyrama Station home, 170 km from Wentworth. Police also found pornographic photos of Miss Larcombe in Suckling's car. They were taken before February 1988. A dress believed to belong to the missing woman was recovered from Suckling, as was a notebook with an entry 'Jodie 27.12'. Suckling was then charged and subsequently committed for trial on murder charges by Magistrate Derek Hand. The DPP then dropped the charges.

Mr Blanch said that Magistrate Hand had accepted what he termed 'a similar fact' in that on 3 March

Daryl Francis Suckling

1988, Suckling forced a woman to take large amounts of alcohol then 'handcuffed her in his vehicle, removed her clothing and placed a chain around her neck and took her to a country property where he lived. He kept her in a drugged state, taking photos of her and raping her'. As we already know, the woman, Sophie Carni, escaped and Suckling was charged with sexual assault and wrongful imprisonment. Suckling was acquitted when Ms Carni died of a drug overdose before Suckling's trial.

Mr Blanch correctly ruled that in the absence of any evidence as to what happened to Jodie Larcombe, it would be 'to a large extent supposition' that she was treated in the same, or in a similar fashion.

The decision to drop the charges against Suckling was made because the evidence against him was weak. He had obviously been with Jodie Larcombe sometime before she disappeared, because 'he took pornographic photographs of her and items of her personal property were found in his possession'.

But 'it was still arguable as to when it was he was with her', and although in February 1988, other photos on the roll of film were taken, there was no date on the pornographic photos, and there was no purchase date on the dress.

As the DPP said: 'It is for the prosecution to prove beyond reasonable doubt that he is guilty – it is not for him to prove he is innocent. ... On the evidence which could be expected to be admitted in a court there is no case against the defendant to be prosecuted. I agree with the two other Queen's Counsel who have examined this matter and have come up with the same conclusion.'

Mysterious Death of Jodie Larcombe

But the police who had worked tirelessly piecing the evidence against Suckling together, did not agree that the case should be dropped. They believed that they had enough on Suckling to convict him. And, understandably, so did Jodie Larcombe's parents.

As harsh as it seemed at the time, the decision would turn out to be the right one, and in the end, the Director of Public Prosecutions, the police and the dead woman's family would get their man.

In late 1991, Jodie Larcombe's parents collected thousands of signatures on a petition calling for the prosecution of the man who had been charged with the murder of their daughter. 'We will fight this in every way and hope someone will sit up and take notice,' Mr Larcombe said.

But despite their tireless efforts to bring their daughter's suspected killer to justice, it wasn't until 2 June 1994 that their prayers were answered when Suckling, then 58, was again charged with the murder of Jodie Larcombe.

Suckling had fallen for the oldest trap of them all. He couldn't keep his mouth shut. In 1994, while in prison serving 6 years for fraud, he had made the fatal mistake of boasting to a cellmate about the abduction and murder of Jodie Larcombe.

The cellmate went to the police, who wired him up with listening devices and recorded Suckling's confessions. This time the DPP decided to prosecute.

On 2 September 1996, Daryl Francis Suckling was jailed for the term of his natural life for abducting, raping, murdering and dismembering Jodie Larcombe, 22, on or about 27 December 1987, at an unknown place in NSW. Her body has never been found.

Daryl Francis Suckling

In sentencing Suckling, Justice Bruce James said that the murder was a horrendous crime in the worst category.

Suckling, the man who had beaten abduction, rape, wrongful imprisonment and murder charges because Sophie Carni died of a drug overdose, was at last behind bars forever.

Chapter 17

Brendan and Vester Fernando

Murder in the Outback

The brutal abduction, rape and murder of Sandra Hoare was an outrage that could have been commonplace in New York or South Africa, but in Australia it didn't seem likely that such a thing could ever happen.

The victim was a nurse, alone on duty in a ward in an outback hospital, caring for a geriatric man. Two young men entered the ward, bashed her elderly patient in front of her, marched her from the hospital at the point of a machete, forced her to undress, sexually assaulted her and then murdered her in cold blood some time between 1.30 and 3.00 am on Friday, 9 December 1994.

It was a crime that would see the two young offenders go to prison for life with the recommendation that they never be released and would bring the northwestern NSW country town of Walgett to the brink of a race war ... whites against blacks.

The fact that the murder victim was the fiance of one of the local policemen didn't help matters. As it was, the powder keg that was about to explode was averted by scores of police descending on Walgett from

Brendan and Vester Fernando

surrounding districts; they were aware of the violence that could erupt at any second and were keen to lock up the murderers as quickly as possible and avoid further bloodshed.

Fortunately, this approach worked. Within two days the murderers were behind bars. Walgett stopped and asked the question: 'How could such a thing happen in our town?'

The murder brought together two cultures that were usually, unfortunately, miles apart. A beautiful, university-trained young woman who had chosen to dedicate her life to healing the sick, and two drug and alcohol-addled young men with long histories of drug abuse, petrol sniffing, violent crime and prison terms.

It was the formula for a disaster of the worst possible kind.

The murdered nurse, Sandra Hoare, was a kind and caring young woman who came from a close family. She had arrived in Walgett a month before her murder and lived with her fiance David Taylor in his flat at the police barracks. Taylor had been posted to Walgett police station a year earlier.

Sandra Hoare had just completed her Bachelor of Nursing degree at the University of Western Sydney and had been working some shifts without pay at Walgett Hospital to gain practical experience while waiting for her Registered Nurse's certificate to come through.

The night she was murdered, Sandra Hoare was working only her second paid shift. She had started work at 11.00 pm.

The lives of her killers, cousins Vester Fernando, 24, and Brendan Fernando, 23, couldn't have been more different. They were a pair of poorly-educated alcoholics; Brendan Fernando's frequent use of drugs such as marijuana and heroin, and the sniffing of petrol and glue, were thought to have brought about the brain damage which left him with an IQ of around 60.

Brendan Fernando had been using marijuana since he was ten years old and alcohol since he was 16, and started sniffing glue in jail when he was 19. When he was arrested for Sandra Hoare's murder, he was using half a gram of heroin a day, smoking marijuana, constantly drinking alcohol and taking up to seven Serapax tranquillisers a day.

Vester Fernando was an alcoholic by the time he turned 16. Both Brendan and Vester Fernando had extensive criminal records that included robbery with violence, and both had served jail terms.

Sadly, the Fernando cousins are typical of many of the Aboriginal people in eastern Australian country towns; the white feller's booze and drugs have taken over and seen to it that too many of the Aboriginal population spend their lives in a disoriented state. This has a disruptive effect on the whole town, creating friction between the Aboriginal and white populations.

Walgett is no different, and it is said of the town that the main *employment* there is *unemployment*, which runs at close to the highest level in Australia. The town's two hotels, the Oasis and the Imperial, in Walgett's main street, are the watering holes for the local Aboriginal community, which makes up about 70% of the population. Very few have jobs and the rest live on Social Security. Payments increase with each additional child, and there are lots of big families out Walgett way.

Brendan and Vester Fernando

No white man in his right mind would go into these pubs for a drink – not unless he was looking for trouble, that is – and especially not on a Thursday night. Thursday night is known locally as 'fight night' because it is Social Security payment day, and a lot of the Aboriginal population is cashed-up, full of firewater, raring to go and looking for trouble.

On the night of Thursday, 8 December 1994, Vester and Brendan Fernando were looking for trouble. Brendan had started drinking with relatives and friends at his mother Iris's home in the late morning and by 6.30 pm he was very drunk. He went into town, where he continued drinking.

Later that night, Brendan met up with his cousin Vester, who had driven in earlier that evening from nearby Brewarrina, where he had spent six weeks at a drying-out centre. He was making the most of his arrival back in Walgett with a long drinking session at the Imperial Hotel.

By the time they teamed up, just after the pub closed, both were very drunk. They spent some time sitting together drinking beer. They went back to Brendan's wooden bungalow on the western side of town and smoked a couple of marijuana joints before returning to town.

At around 11.30 pm, Vester became very aggressive, which often happened when he had been drinking. He produced a long-handled machete and held it to the throat of an Aboriginal youth, threatening to kill him.

Vester eventually let the youth go unharmed but the incident would later play an important part in the swift apprehension of Sandra Hoare's killers.

Murder in the Outback

The Fernando cousins then wandered the streets looking for more to drink. At about 1.00 am they approached a youth and invited him to steal a car from the Walgett Hospital car park with them. The youth declined. They decided to steal a car anyway, a mistake that would cost them the rest of their lives.

As Brendan and Vester Fernando broke into a blue Sigma station wagon in the hospital car park, they noticed Sandra Hoare observing them through the window of the Peg Cross Geriatric Ward. She was alone on duty and attending to an elderly patient.

Brendan went into the hospital to 'check on her'. Vester gained access to the ward by another door, bashed the elderly patient and abducted the nurse at machete point. In pitch darkness, they forced her to walk to a nearby oval, where she was bashed and stripped and Vester sexually assaulted her while Brendan held her legs.

Half-naked, Sandra Hoare was then marched another 400 metres to another paddock where Vester hit her in the neck with the long handled machete, killing her and almost decapitating her. In his evidence, Brendan said that he heard Sandra Hoare scream once.

Immediately after the nurse was sbducted, police were informed by the elderly patient that he had been bashed by two black men and that Sandra Hoare was missing. They mounted a massive search. A police helicopter crew found her body near a paddock fence the following afternoon.

She was dressed only in her nurse's blue uniform slacks, and she was partially buried in the soil, the huge wound in her neck obviously made by someone with an axe ... or a machete.

Brendan and Vester Fernando

In the meantime, the extra police in Walgett were raiding Aboriginal camps and houses and rounding up and questioning Aboriginal people, sometimes at the point of a gun, in their search for the killers.

Their break came when the youth who had been threatened the previous evening by Vester Fernando with his double-handed machete came forward and told them what had happened.

Brendan Fernando was arrested almost immediately. He told police everything they needed to know. He didn't hesitate to incriminate Vester. He denied taking part in the actual rape and claimed he was walking away from the scene of the crime when Vester killed the young nurse with the machete.

When Vester was picked up two days after the murder, at his sister's house in Dubbo, 300 km away, he claimed to have heard about the murder but not to have any idea who did it.

He claimed to have been in bed, asleep, at Walgett when the murder was taking place, and he refused to give samples of his blood or hair for scientific examination.

Although Vester never confessed to murdering the young woman, police considered that there was more than enough circumstantial evidence to charge him with the murder of Sandra Hoare. There was the young man he had confronted with the machete in Walgett. A similar machete was found in the exact spot where Brendan told police he had seen Vester hiding it. Vester was in possession of cassette tapes that had been taken from the blue Sigma station wagon that they had broken into in the hospital car park. And finally, there was the evidence of his cousin Brendan, who had witnessed the crime.

It would prove to be more than enough to convict him of murder.

Many considered that the brain-damaged Brendan would receive leniency from the court in view of the fact that he had been co-operative with police from the outset, and because he steadfastly maintained that he was walking away from the murder scene when Vester struck the fatal blow.

But that was not to be the case. He was charged with 'acting in a joint criminal enterprise' with his cousin Vester, and was convicted of murder along with Vester after the prosecution pointed out that legally, it did not matter who struck the fatal blow or blows to Ms Hoare.

'The Crown says the two accused were there to kill this girl. Both were present, one or both of them striking blows to the girl's body,' the prosecution had argued.

In a brave show of family solidarity, Sandra Hoare's mother, Pauline Hoare, accompanied by family members, had attended the trial each day wearing lapel badges with Sandra's face on them.

After the jury took two and a half hours in the Supreme Court at Darlinghurst to find both men guilty, the trial judge, Justice Alan Abadee, said that there was no doubt in his mind that Vester Fernando used the machete to kill Sandra Hoare and that Brendan Fernando had held the young nurse's legs while Vester had sexually assaulted her.

And although Brendan Fernando vigorously denied it, the judge said that he believed, on the evidence, that Brendan had held the woman while the murder took place.

Brendan and Vester Fernando

The judge was not moved by expert witnesses who testified that after extensive tests on Brendan Fernando, that they had concluded that he had a low IQ and was more than likely brain-damaged from his years of heroin use, alcohol abuse and sniffing petrol and glue.

On the subject of rehabilitation, defence lawyers agreed that should he (Justice Abadee) sentence the Fernando cousins to a life in prison, the young men would have little or no prospect of rehabilitation.

Justice Abadee dismissed the defence's claims by saying that rehabilitation for the cousins 'seems to me to be almost idealistic nonsense'.

Justice Abadee also listened to the defence lawyers' arguments that Aboriginal people in towns such as Walgett often went on heavy drinking binges and that their clients' drunken condition at the time of the murder should be taken into consideration when he came to sentencing the young men.

Justice Abadee replied to this by asking why alcohol should be blamed any more in the cases of Aboriginal defendants than in cases where the offenders were members of any other ethnic group.

At their sentencing on 21 August 1997, Justice Abadee said that Vester Fernando almost decapitated Ms Hoare with a machete. There were signs that it had been used like a saw — back and forth across her neck. Several cuts on her face and neck were probably inflicted before she died.

'There was extended concentrated suffering over a period of an hour or so,' Justice Abadee said. 'There was accompanying degradation and humiliation. The injuries to the jaw and face caused by the use of the machete, being a form of physical torture, ought not to be overlooked. There is the mental torture, terror and great fear. Next, this is a case [of] two strong men killing a young, defenceless and vulnerable woman who had done them no harm.

'Each has served prison sentences. Neither has learned from his experience,' Justice Abadee said in sentencing Brendan and Vester Fernando to life in prison with the recommendation that they never be released. He added that he was 'deeply conscious' of their relative youth and that each was likely to spend at least 50 years in jail, but that that was the 'grim reality'.

The sentencing made the Fernando cousins unique in the Australian prison system in two ways: they are the first Aboriginal people ever sentenced to 'never be released', and Brendan, at age 23 and Vester, at age 24, are the youngest prisoners in the system who have been sentenced to die in jail.

Brendan and Vester Fernando appealed their convictions and the sentence that was given. The hearing before the Court of Criminal Appeal has been completed but, as at the date of publication, judgment has not been delivered.

Chapter 18

RICHARD WILLIAM LEONARD

The Bow and Arrow Butcher

Within three months of Denise Shipley moving in to live with her lover, Richard Leonard, he had shown her a dismembered human body he kept in his freezer in two garbage bags.

When bored, Leonard rolled the head across the floor and rearranged the arms around it on the floor, pretending they were part of a jigsaw puzzle.

They were the frozen remains of a young homosexual man whom Leonard had shot through the heart with a powerful bow and arrow and dismembered. The murder took place three weeks before he and Shipley had met again, rekindling an old acquaintanceship – when they were kids, they had gone to church together.

Shipley's devotion to the killer would eventually lead her to prison. Leonard would be sentenced to spend the rest of his life behind bars, his papers marked 'never to be released'.

Richard Leonard killed two men in separate barbaric homicides, and on both occasions Shipley helped him cover his tracks. This included helping Leonard dispose of his first victim's (Mr Dempsey) body parts; she had thought they were frozen fish for the first period of their relationship.

The Bow and Arrow Butcher

Richard William Leonard came from a middle-class, born-again Christian family and grew up in and around the lush waterways of Pittwater, in Sydney's north. Throughout his teen years he regularly attended services at the Collaroy Plateau Christian Worship Centre and the Mona Vale Christian Life Centre with his family.

His well-respected father, Stephen Leonard, ran a successful shipbuilding business and Richard was the eldest of Janet and Stephen Leonard's family of two boys and three girls. It was a kind, loving, deeply religious family.

Richard grew up in an environment that he loved – the lush Australian outdoors near the family home on the fringe of Sydney's northern national parks – and he developed a passion for snakes and taxidermy. He would often bring home dead animals and put them in the fridge to be cut up and examined later.

Richard Leonard was described as a talented lad with a genius IQ, and if there was anything in his past to indicate that he would grow into a monster, it was the annual visits to his paternal grandmother at her home in Buderim in Queensland. The Leonard family spent the long summer holidays there.

In evidence at his trial it was alleged that it was here that Leonard was taught by his grandmother, Silvia Levi, how to torture and mutilate live kittens by cutting off their ears and tails.

When he left school, Richard took an apprenticeship in shipbuilding in the family business. He also worked for a time at an abattoir in Inverell cutting up carcasses – a craft that would come in handy later, when he went about dismembering his first murder victim.

Richard William Leonard

It was at the Christian Life Centre that Richard Leonard first met Denise Shipley; he was 15 and she was 13. Denise was a student at the Northern Beaches Christian School and Richard was attending Cromer High School.

They developed a friendly relationship but drifted apart when the church forbade them from seeing each other because of their ages.

Things went drastically wrong with Richard Leonard's life when he left home, at 17, and moved in with a drug-dealing relative. It was here that Richard was introduced to a deadly cocktail of mind-altering drugs such as speed, angel dust, LSD and cocaine, all of which he started using very heavily.

Within months Leonard had moved into another house – the drugs flowed so freely there that he likened the place to a 'drug supermarket'. His family and friends noticed that his once effervescent personality was deteriorating dramatically as the increased drug use took its toll on his young body and mind.

Aware of Richard's plight and desperate to get him out of the bad company he was keeping, Stephen Leonard sent his son to stay with an uncle overseas, but when the young man returned to Australia he went straight back into drugs. Once again, his appearance deteriorated rapidly.

Richard Leonard moved into a tiny bedsitter by himself at Warriewood, still in Sydney's north. By now, fuelled with a mixture of drugs, he had developed a passion for extreme violence and black magic – sick fantasies bordering on necrophilia and the ritualistically macabre.

With his high-powered bow and arrows Leonard

The Bow and Arrow Butcher

hunted mullet in nearby Deep Creek, well-known as a homosexual haunt.

In late 1993, Leonard aimed an arrow at two men as they walked along a bush path. One of the men jumped into the bushes, terrified, and Leonard quickly transferred his aim to the other man, who ran off. He returned with a large tree branch and confronted his aggressor.

Leonard put the bow and arrow away and laughed off the incident, claiming that he was just joking.

But he wasn't joking. On 2 August 1994, a few days before his twenty-first birthday, when he fired an arrow into the heart of Stephen Richard Dempsey, a 34-year-old New Zealand landscape gardener who, Leonard would claim later, approached him for sex. Dempsey was killed instantly.

Leonard threw Dempsey's body into the creek. He returned later that evening with a boning knife and dismembered the body. He then wrapped the body pieces in garbage bags and took them home to the freezer. It took several trips on his motorbike to do this.

A few weeks after he had stored Dempsey's body in the freezer, Denise Shipley, then 18, came to visit. She ended up moving in shortly after. They had bumped into each other quite by accident a few weeks earlier and discovered that the flame they had lit during their early teens had never really gone out.

The eldest of three children, the thin, attractive, dark-haired Shipley was unemployed, experimenting with drugs and had recently appeared in court on dishonesty charges. She had been fined $600 and placed on a 12-month good behaviour bond. Moving out of her parents' home looked like a good option, so

Richard William Leonard

meeting and moving in with Leonard was the perfect answer.

It was a liaison that would result in disaster for Denise Shipley.

On 18 November 1994, Shipley and Leonard caught a cab from the city to Collaroy Plateau while they were tripping on LSD. They had no money and their game plan was to bolt when the cab pulled up near where they lived.

But instead of doing a runner, Leonard produced a long-bladed boning knife and held it to the throat of the driver, 42-year-old father of seven, Ezzedine Bahmad. The brave cab driver fought Leonard off and grabbed at the knife in an attempt to save himself, but the young man overpowered him and stabbed him to death in a wild frenzy. Bahmad's autopsy revealed that he had been stabbed 37 times and his throat had been slashed three times by the razor-sharp knife.

Leonard and Shipley left the cabbie dead on the front seat. Shipley did nothing to prevent the murder and did not attempt to help the stricken taxi driver as he fought for his life. Later it would be alleged that she assisted Leonard by turning the taxi's engine off so the driver couldn't take off.

During the wild attack, Leonard was wounded and the couple sought medical assistance at St Vincent's Hospital. Leonard explained his collapsed lung to doctors and police at the hospital by claiming that they had been set upon by an Asian gang in a park.

Hospital staff noted, and would tell police later, that the young man had refused anaesthetic and seemed to experience pleasure in the pain of having a tube inserted in his chest.

The Bow and Arrow Butcher

Paranoid that police were onto them and now allegedly terrified of Leonard, who was talking about making a film about a necrophiliac hero who murders a cab driver, Shipley demanded that he get rid of the dismembered body in the freezer. In early December 1994, she helped her lover weigh the body parts down with rocks, wrap them in chicken wire and dump them in Pittwater.

When Mr Dempsey's torso (the rest of the body parts were never found) washed up nearby a few weeks later, with an arrow wound to the chest, baffled police appealed to the general public for help.

They received many calls, including one from the two men whom Leonard had aimed the bow and arrow at in late 1993. Several of these calls pointed towards Richard Leonard – he owned a high-powered bow and arrow and, from all accounts, was more than capable of committing murder and dismembering a body.

Police did some digging on Leonard and a check of the hospitals revealed that he had been treated for a stab wound on the same night that a cab driver had been murdered near where he and the young lady who had taken him to hospital lived.

The net was closing as police began to work out the link between the two homicides.

When confronted by police about their whereabouts on the nights of the murders, the pair denied any knowledge of the crimes. Shipley changed her story about Leonard being stabbed by an Asian gang and instead said that Leonard had been accidentally stabbed while the pair were indulging in a sadomasochistic sex session in nearby Hyde Park.

Richard William Leonard

Unable to lay any charges, but convinced that Leonard and Shipley were guilty, police bugged their apartment and kept them under surveillance while they built up a case against them.

Blood samples other than the taxi driver's were found in the taxi and Leonard and Shipley were asked to provide both blood and hair samples to see if they matched.

The couple judged, correctly, that police were catching up with them, and in late April 1995 they decided to shake the police off by constantly moving around. Using money that Leonard had made working as a security guard and that Shipley had made working as a prostitute, they moved from one luxury hotel to another, ate in the best restaurants and got stoned on a cocktail of illegal drugs.

At the height of their revelry they bought two silver rings from a flea market and went through a form of marriage by themselves, exchanging vows in a room at the luxurious Sebel Townhouse in Sydney.

On 3 May 1995, Leonard and Shipley spoke to a priest at the Christian City Church at Brookvale and gave themselves up to detectives.

At his trial, Richard Leonard pleaded not guilty to Dempsey's murder, claiming that on the day of Stephen Dempsey's death he (Leonard) was at Deep Creek catching mullet with his compound bow and metal broad head arrows when Mr Dempsey approached him for unwanted sex. He claimed he had been provoked, and had killed Dempsey in self defence.

The prosecution argued that Leonard had gone to Deep Creek knowing it was a homosexual meeting

The Bow and Arrow Butcher

place, with the sole purpose of killing another human being with his deadly bow and arrow.

The fact that immediately after he had killed him, Leonard stored the deceased's body in the cool waters of Deep Creek, knowing from his days working in the abattoir that this made a carcass easier to cut up later, and returned later that evening, dismembered the body, took it home in plastic bags and stored them in the freezer, was proof that he was a premeditated cold-blooded killer, the court was told.

The court was also told that Leonard suffered from a very severe and extreme personality disorder that began in his early childhood years when he spent holidays with his paternal grandmother, Silvia Levi. Leonard's own family backed up these shocking allegations and, speaking of Silvia Levi, who had confirmed the assertions before she died in 1997, Richard Leonard's mother Janet said: 'She was a free spirit with her own ideas about bringing up children. Over a 10-year period she had him (Leonard) in her care, looking after him during major school holidays. At the age of 70, she may have made the mistake with his aggression with animals and let him go too far before she stopped it. It is up to an adult to stop a child.'

Having little going for him at his eight-day trial, held in late 1997, Leonard tried to give the impression that it was he, Leonard, who was in fact the victim of an unwanted homosexual advance, but the facade came crashing down around him when the prosecution revealed a damning insight into Leonard's real character by playing a taped conversation of Leonard talking about his case to his cellmate in May 1996, while he was awaiting trial.

Richard William Leonard

Pretending that he had contacted Stephen Dempsey in the spirit-world, Leonard had a make-believe conversation with the deceased man and laughed and joked as he recalled killing him, saying: 'What do you want to tell me? Fuck you. You telling me to get fucked? You know what, you're just a putrid fucking faggie, you know I really enjoyed knocking you, you fucking piece of shit.'

Describing the actual killing of Dempsey to his cellmate as 'really funny', Leonard went on to say that the look on Dempsey's face as the arrow struck him in the heart was like 'he can't fucking believe it's happening. It's like, oh fuck, I can't believe it's come to this'.

It still took the jury four days of deliberation to find Leonard guilty of murder, but any doubts that any of the jurors may have had were soon dispelled. Shortly after they had announced their guilty verdict, they were told that on the very day that they were empanelled, Leonard had pleaded guilty to the stabbing murder of taxi driver Ezzedine Bahmad.

Justice Jeremy Badgery-Parker said he agreed with the experts who said that Leonard was a psychopath with little hope of successful treatment. 'I regard the prospects of rehabilitation as only slight, and given the magnitude of the danger which he presents to the community today, I am persuaded beyond reasonable doubt that there will be a risk of him committing further crimes of violence upon release, if ever he should be released,' he said.

In sentencing Leonard on 10 November 1997 to the maximum penalty – life imprisonment – on both charges of murder, Justice Badgery-Parker said Leonard

The Bow and Arrow Butcher

took pleasure in his murders and was too dangerous to ever be released from jail. The sentence made him the twelfth person in NSW to be jailed for the term of his natural life under the 1989 truth-in-sentencing legislation.

As he was led from the court to spend the rest of his life behind bars, Richard Leonard couldn't resist the temptation of one last defiant act of dominance over one of the victims he had left in the wake of his carnage.

He turned and winked at Lulu Dempsey, the mother of Stephen Dempsey, the man he had murdered and dismembered and stored in his freezer.

At her trial, which ended on 19 November 1997, a Supreme Court jury found Denise Shipley not guilty of the murder of taxi driver Ezzedine Bahmad, but guilty of being an accessory after the fact.

Justice Badgery-Parker sentenced Shipley to a minimum of 3 years and a maximum of 8 years for her part in Leonard's crimes. The judge said Shipley had shown genuine remorse and a willingness to rehabilitate herself.

Chapter 19

PAUL WADE STREETON

The Crime that Touched Australia's Heart

'I wanted people in society to feel the pain that I was going through. I wanted to punish people for ruining my life.'

These were the reasons Paul Wade Streeton gave for pouring petrol over a boy in a Cairns school playground and igniting him.

But his feeble and cowardly excuses did not impress the judge, Justice Margaret White who, in the Queensland Supreme Court in Cairns in March 1997, sentenced Streeton, a 27-year-old charity worker from Adelaide, to life imprisonment with no fixed non-parole period for attempted murder – the equivalent of 'never to be released'.

In doing so, Justice White bestowed upon Streeton the dubious honour of becoming only the second person (at the time) in modern Australian history to be jailed for the term of his natural life for a crime other than murder. (The other case was that of Robert Raymond Day, who was sentenced to life and had his papers marked 'never to be released' for the attempted murder of a Danish tourist in 1990. Since then, another person has been sent to jail 'never to be released' for a

The Crime that Touched Australia's Heart

crime other than murder – Wing Piew Chung, for drug dealing, in 1998. Both cases are covered in this book.)

On 10 October 1996, at 1.40 pm, schoolchildren watched in horror as a man carrying a 5-litre can of petrol in a bag walked into their playground, poured petrol all over 6-year-old Aboriginal boy Tjandamurra O'Shane, a Year 1 student, and set him on fire with a cigarette lighter.

The man then casually walked out of the schoolyard and surrendered himself to a traffic policeman on duty outside the school.

The school principal, Michael Aitken, rushed to the boy's aid and smothered the flames with his shirt and his hand and rolled the boy over and over on the ground to put out the flames. Mr Aitken suffered burns to one hand and part of his leg, but he undoubtedly saved the boy's life.

Jenni Joseph, a teacher at the school, said she was sitting in the staffroom when another teacher ran in to fill a bucket of water and told them that a child was on fire in the playground. The stricken child was lying on the ground crying, surrounded by adults putting out the flames with the water.

With burns to 70% of his little body, Tjandamurra was flown to the Royal Children's Hospital in Brisbane. By late that night, he was in a critical condition and not expected to live.

But brave little Tjandamurra O'Shane would live, and would become a symbol of courage for all Australians.

And while Tjandamurra was in hospital fighting for his life, Cairns police were trying to piece together

Paul Wade Streeton

what happened and, more importantly, why it happened.

From what police could gather, Paul Wade Streeton was a charity collector for an organisation in SA, and had been reported missing by his employer a few days before the torching of the boy. He had been in Cairns for only a week.

After questioning Streeton, police were convinced that the attack was not politically or racially motivated and that Streeton did not know the boy or his family. He had no interest in, nor held any strong views on, politics.

Streeton entered no plea when he appeared in the Cairns Magistrates' Court on 11 October, the day following the attack, charged with attempted murder and attempted grievous bodily harm. He did not apply for bail and was remanded in custody to appear again on 11 December 1996.

In the meantime, all of Australia was relieved to hear that the little boy Streeton set ablaze was alive and that his 'critical' listing had been changed to 'serious but stable'. It looked as though he might survive the ordeal.

Tjandamurra's uncle, Terry O'Shane, said Australia 'should take a bow for the warmth and compassion it has shown to the trauma his family had been through in the past few days'. He said that the following day would be the decider in knowing if Tjandamurra would pull through or not, and added: 'The doctors said if he can pull through until then, there's a good chance. He will fight on.'

'We have had so much help from so many people, even from overseas. We had calls from England and I received $150 from some local workers. It has been incredible; it has given us so much strength.

The Crime that Touched Australia's Heart

'We live at Halloways Beach. It's just a small place,' Terry O'Shane said. 'The local newsagent put a box out last night to get some funds to help us out. There was $100 in it this morning. That's the type of response we're getting.'

And as the news programs around the nation relayed the story, Tjandamurra's aunt, the highly respected Pat O'Shane, Australia's first Aboriginal magistrate, was on her way from Sydney to join Tjandamurra's parents, Jenny and Tim, in a bedside vigil at the hospital in Brisbane. All of Australia prayed that the little boy with the big heart would pull through.

Although still in a serious condition, on 14 October, just four days after he was set alight, doctors performed the first of what would become many skin grafts on Tjandamurra.

By 19 October, Tjandamurra was being prepared for his second skin graft and had received telegrams from the Prime Minister, John Howard, and the Queensland Premier, Bob Borbidge, and had been paid a visit by Olympic athlete Cathy Freeman.

Still unable to talk because of the tubes down his throat, and unable to sit up in his special bed (it had a mattress filled with silica sand to help him feel as if he was floating, not lying down), the condition of the brave little boy who had a nation cheering for him improved every day.

Around about the time that Paul Wade Streeton appeared in the Cairns Magistrates' Court on 11 December 1996, and had his trial date set for March 1997, Tjandamurra O'Shane was having his ninth and final skin graft before starting rehabilitation. He would remain heavily bandaged and in his infection-controlled room for another four to six weeks.

The national newspapers gave almost daily reports of Tjandamurra's progress and masses of letters of support and gifts flowed in from all over the country.

By the time Streeton was about to face trial for his crime, in March 1997, Tjandamurra was at home with his family and playing his guitar, clothed in a hot, restrictive pressure suit – it covers every inch of his body except for his face and ears. He will have to wear the suit for two years.

At his trial, Streeton pleaded guilty to grievous bodily harm with intent, but not guilty to the charge of attempted murder.

In a taped interview played to the court, Streeton said that he had been planning such an attack since he was in Year 2 and wanted the death penalty for his crime. He said that he had chosen a child as he (Streeton) was only slightly built and he wanted his attack to succeed.

He explained that the attack was his way of 'getting out', because he didn't want to live any more. He said that he had never attempted suicide because he was squeamish and frightened of sharp objects.

'I dread existing without the success I deserve,' he said in the interview. He said that he wanted to pay back an education system which had failed to recognise his intelligence.

He also claimed that his parents had let him down and betrayed him when teachers had suggested he lacked intelligence. 'I want people to be aware [of] what I am angry about. I couldn't see any other solution to my predicament. I have nothing against the child. I just wanted to hurt those people who make me feel unsafe and threatened.'

When asked if he was aware that he could have killed the boy, he replied, 'I suppose I knew I could have killed him. I didn't have any preference between killing him and hurting him.'

The Prosecutor, John Bailey, told the court how Streeton had 'calmly, coldly and wickedly' walked up to children playing tiggy (tag) in the schoolyard at lunchtime, singled Tjandamurra out, poured petrol all over him and set it alight.

Bailey said Streeton was a 'bitter, selfish and self-centred person' who then turned himself over to police, asking for the death penalty. 'This proved that he had murder on his mind,' he said.

After a two-day trial, it took the jury five hours to reject Streeton's argument that he did not intend to murder Tjandamurra O'Shane.

In sentencing Streeton, Justice Margaret White was scornful of his cowardly act and said that Streeton had shown 'not one moment of remorse or regret for his actions and still referred to his victim as "it".'

Justice White sentenced Streeton to prison with no recommendation for a non-parole period.

In late 1996, Channel 7's Witness program set up the O'Shane Family Appeal, and by March 1997, more than $65,000 had been raised.

Tjandamurra O'Shane is a living source of inspiration to all Australians.

Paul Wade Streeton is in protective custody. He lives in constant fear for his life.

Chapter 20

EARL HEATLEY

Natural Born Lifer

In 1966, a remorseless 19-year-old Earl Heatley admitted to police that he had murdered 22-year-old Robert Francis Dunn because Dunn threw a bottle at his car as he drove past, and hurled abuse at him.

In retaliation, Heatley went home and picked up his rifle, came back to the car park in Granville, Sydney, and shot and killed Dunn. Heatley was sentenced to life imprisonment, but after serving 15 years, he was released in 1981 – to commit murder again.

This time he would kill two men, one his own brother, in the bungled robbery of a factory that contained no money or valuables. And again, as in his first killing all those years ago, Heatley, now a middle-aged, grey-haired 51-year-old, would not show a skerrick of regret as he was ushered off to jail for the rest of his life.

Heatley and his brother, Paul, went to a warehouse in Asquith, on the outskirts of Sydney, in October 1994, with the intention of robbing the premises of legal, but very hard to acquire, chemicals required in the making of amphetamines. Earl Heatley was armed with a pistol and wore a mask.

They marched factory cleaner Thomas Alan Bithell into another part of the factory to confront the factory owner Des Thompson who, having seen what was going on, was on the phone, apparently to the police.

Paul Heatley charged into Thompson's office, punched him in the face and tried to rip the phone out of the wall. But it would not yield. Paul Heatley panicked and called for his brother to run away, telling him that the police were on their way.

As Paul Heatley started to run away he was tackled by 67-year-old Mr Thompson who, even though he was 20 years older than Heatley, managed to get the better of him and hold him.

Paul Heatley called to his brother Earl to 'shoot him, shoot him, shoot him'. These were to be his final words. Earl Heatley opened fire on the pair, sending four bullets into Des Thompson's head and body. One of the bullets passed through Thompson's body and fatally wounded Paul Heatley.

Earl Heatley then put four more bullets into Thompson's head as he lay on the ground dying and would tell police later that he did it because Thompson was 'lying there crying like a dog, so I put four bullets in his head'.

Paul Heatley staggered to the outside of the factory, where he fell to the ground and died.

During the shooting, the cleaner was wounded by a bullet which entered his forearm and disintegrated as it shattered the bone.

Earl Heatley was arrested and charged with two counts of murder and one of malicious wounding. He pleaded not guilty on all counts but the evidence against him was overwhelming.

At his trial, before Justice McInerney in the NSW Supreme Court in February 1998, Earl Heatley offered

Earl Heatley

no evidence that could help his case. He also refused to give the names of the drug manufacturers he and his brother were stealing the ingredients for. In return, the court showed him no mercy.

Earl Heatley was sentenced to die in jail for the murder of Des Thompson. He became the fourteenth person in NSW to be sentenced to spend the rest of his life behind bars under the 1989 truth-in-sentencing legislation.

Earl Heatley was also sentenced to 35 years for killing his brother and maliciously wounding Thomas Alan Bithell.

Chapter 21

WING PIEW CHUNG

The End of 'Mr Smack'

Singaporean national Wing Piew Chung found Australia a paradise in which to sell his deadly heroin. Business was brilliant; so good, in fact, that the multi-millionaire Chung had to increase the amounts he was bringing in – he was believed to have imported and sold as much as $500 million dollars' worth of the deadly narcotic in a two-year period.

Chung, 44, was a high-ranking member of the Ah Kong (derived from the Chinese word Kongsi, meaning company or co-operative), a drug trafficking organisation that competes internationally with the Chinese Triads.

Found guilty in the NSW District Court in April 1998 of supplying 63 kg of high-grade heroin with a street value of almost $150 million, Chung is the first narcotics trafficker to be sentenced to life imprisonment under the NSW Drugs Misuse and Trafficking Act. A life sentence under this Act is also subject to the 1989 NSW truth-in-sentencing legislation, so this prisoner will never be released.

Little is known about Chung's background except that he served a 7-year jail term in Singapore in the '70s. He set up a network of heroin traffickers and dealers throughout Sydney in the early to mid-'90s, and for several years dominated the Australian heroin market.

Chung was reputedly very dangerous, and would let nothing interfere with his heroin trafficking. It was alleged that he had murdered two drug rivals in Amsterdam in the early '80s and shot another man dead in Bangkok in 1985.

His background in murder and narcotics eventually led him into the lucrative Australian market, where he set up a network so big that it would temporarily put the traditional Chinese heroin traffickers out of business.

But Chung's heroin importing didn't always run smoothly. In 1994, 124 kg of pure heroin was dumped overboard from a fishing vessel in Darwin in a badly botched importation attempt.

But even when the heroin did flow freely, Chung had the constant worry of where to keep it safe from the police. One of his hiding spots was a room in an exclusive inner Sydney apartment building, where an around-the-clock team had to guard up to 14 kg of heroin at a time, never letting it out of their sight until it was distributed to the dealers.

Sydney's theatre complexes and restaurants became the dropping off and picking up points for Chung's army of dealers, and big bags of cash would be swapped for packages of almost pure heroin.

From there it would be broken down time and again until it wound up in the arms of the junkies in places such as Cabramatta in Sydney's west and Kings Cross in the inner-city red light district.

Chung left Australia in the mid-'90s. On his return in 1996, he was apprehended and charged with supplying the 63 kg of heroin.

The End of 'Mr Smack'

At his trial, Chung offered no defence and called no witnesses. No family members were present in the courtroom. The multi-millionaire narcotics trader seemed resigned to his fate. He was found guilty mainly on the testimony of a fellow member of the Ah Kong gang.

In sentencing Chung, Judge Frederick Kirkham noted the 'human death toll' of young Australians killed by overdoses and contaminated heroin. 'Heroin addiction leads people to rob, cheat and steal,' he said.

'It is from the fruits of these crimes that the money used to buy heroin finds its way into the pockets of large-scale heroin dealers, like the prisoner (Chung). It seems the case [that] while ever large profits are available to be made, people like the prisoner will be prepared to take the risks of detection, prosecution and imprisonment.'

With that, the judge ordered Chung to stand up. 'Having found this case to fall into the 'worst case' category, I am constrained to impose the maximum penalty. You are sentenced to imprisonment for life.'

Chapter 22

GARY ZANE GLASBY

The World's Worst Hit Man

Although it was alleged that Carmela Theissi employed the services of career criminal Gary Glasby and his wife Suzette to murder her husband at Georges Hall in suburban Sydney in 1994 for between $30,000 and $50,000, it was never proven. Carmela Theissi eventually went free while her husband's killers went to prison; Gary Glasby for the rest of his life.

Gary Zane Glasby, 37 at the time, an extremely violent professional who was on a methadone program for his heroin addiction, seemed to be the perfect unbalanced person to carry out a murder.

Unfortunately, Glasby wasn't a very competent criminal, as indicated by his 11-paged conviction sheet. The sheet began when he was thirteen. By the time he was fifteen, he was committing serious criminal offences.

Glasby had been in and out of the toughest jails in NSW for an assortment of offences, including armed robbery with wounding. When his previous girlfriend left him, he burned her mother's house down. Glasby was also charged with the murder of a prisoner at Goulburn prison in 1987, but was acquitted.

Glasby was proud of his anti-social career and achievements. But he was even less successful as a hit

The World's Worst Hit Man

man than he had been at the other criminal ventures he had been involved in.

His pregnant wife of four months, 23-year-old Suzette, was an equally unfortunate human being. Not of high intelligence, she had worked as a prostitute to support her heroin habit and had met Glasby at a methadone clinic. They lived a meagre existence in a caravan in a caravan park at Parklea, in Sydney's western suburbs.

Gary Glasby's only income was his invalid pension. He had had a violent blow to the head the previous year, and it had rendered him unable to work. With not nearly enough money coming in to support their combined drug habits, Glasby subsidised their income with crime.

So when between $30,000 and $50,000 was allegedly on offer to commit murder, the pair jumped at it, thinking little of the consequences.

Their target was an almost equally unfortunate individual, 41-year-old John Theissi. Although John and Carmela Theissi, his wife of 16 years, lived in their own home in Sydney's west where they were raising their three young daughters, and he held down a secure job as a foreman diesel mechanic, he believed that he was some sort of sex god in a world of swingers, wife-swapping and kinky sexual activities.

Unfortunately for John Theissi, he was not a good sort. At just 165 cm tall, he was a thickset, overweight, middle-aged man with a moustache and the sexual appetite of a thoroughbred stud.

And he dressed accordingly, in bright, flecked shirts and shiny trousers. He was the type of guy most women would run a million miles from.

Gary Zane Glasby

John Theissi's favourite fantasy was wife-swapping, but Carmela wasn't even remotely interested in going to wife-swapping parties, let alone pairing off with someone else's partner. This made life a little difficult for the horny swinger.

So when The Close Encounter Erotic Contact Club said in their newsletter that they had lady members who were looking to experience the joys of having two men at once but there was a shortage of eligible, horny blokes, John Theissi thought he had found paradise on Earth, with or without his wife. He applied for the 'job', stating that if he were not accepted as an individual member he and his wife would be only too happy to participate as a couple. Carmela was not impressed.

John Theissi's insistence that his wife join him in sexual encounters with other couples and with some of his mates caused huge rifts in the household, resulting in violent domestic battles. Carmela sought a restraining order against her husband only a few weeks before he was murdered.

It was alleged by Suzette Glasby in court that late in October, Carmela Theissi met briefly with Gary Glasby at McDonald's at Villawood, where she handed him $2000 and left. Suzette alleged that the money was towards having her husband killed but Gary Glasby would claim in court that he was selling stolen gear for Carmela and that he had been framed for the murder.

In the meantime, Gary Glasby, posing as a swinger named 'Steve' who was married to 'Kayla' (Suzette), made contact with John Theissi and indicated that his (Steve's) wife was willing to have sex with him (Theissi). Naturally, John Theissi was obliging. Glasby arranged a meeting with the unsuspecting Theissi.

The World's Worst Hit Man

On the evening of 6 November 1994, John Theissi met with 'Steve' at a pre-arranged spot. Theissi moved across to the passenger seat of his Range Rover, thus allowing the heavily tattooed man with the unkempt shoulder-length hair to drive him to his death, on the pretext that they were heading for a sexual rendezvous with the man's wife.

What Theissi did not know was that Suzette was following in her car. They headed towards a lover's lane by a local lake. Once there, Gary Glasby didn't waste any time with small talk. He produced a gun, held it to Theissi's head and forced him to kneel on the passenger-side floor of his Range Rover.

But the killing almost didn't happen – even at point blank range, the inept contract killer missed Theissi with the first shot and instead shot out the passenger-side window. Then the gun wouldn't fire. It took two more attempts before a bullet finally made its way into the terrified would-be wife-swapper's brain and he slumped dead on the floor of his car. His body was discovered the following day, wedged underneath the dashboard.

It was too amateurish to be considered a professional hit, and police didn't have to look too far for suspects – the details of the rendezvous with the Glasbys, including their phone number, were found in Theissi's pocket.

Carmela Theissi was very distressed when told of her husband's demise and surmised that it must have been something to do with drugs. No one believed her because, for all of his shortcomings, that was one thing that John Theissi was definitely not involved with.

Police kept a close eye on the Glasbys and Carmela and noted that within days of her husband's death she

Gary Zane Glasby

had a valuation done on the house. They photographed Carmela and Glasby talking together only weeks after the killing. It was explained away later as a chance meeting – they knew each other from when Carmela worked in a hospital.

Police bugged the Glasbys' caravan. What they heard incriminated them both and suggested that Carmela Theissi may have paid them money to have her unfaithful husband murdered. They were all picked up and charged. When Gary Glasby learned of the tapes he allegedly shrugged his shoulders and said: 'Well, that's it. You've got me. That's me fucked.'

Carmela Theissi was committed for trial but the case was no-billed (not proceeded with as the Crown believed they had no chance of winning) when the Director of Public Prosecutions withdrew the indictment after her barrister argued that the tape recording was not evidence and that every other bit of evidence against her was circumstantial.

Suzette Glasby was not so fortunate, and for her part in luring John Theissi to his death on the promise of sex, she was jailed on 11 November 1997 for a minimum of 9 years.

The world's worst hit man, Gary Zane Glasby, also turned out to be the world's most unconvincing witness, and on 11 June 1998, in the NSW Supreme Court, he was sentenced to jail for the term of his natural life, never to be released.

Chapter 23

LINDSEY ROBERT ROSE

The St Valentine's Day Murderer

The bespectacled, heavily manacled 43-year-old man in the dock with the college-boy haircut looked more like his stated occupation of 'former paramedic' and 'Granville Train Disaster hero' than one of Australia's most prolific killers.

Yet Lindsey Robert Rose admitted carrying out five gruesome murders – including killing two women and setting fire to their brothel on St Valentine's Day – in suburban Sydney for money, revenge and robbery, and because the victims were unfortunate enough to be with his intended targets.

Killing in cold blood, for whatever reason, was what Lindsey Rose was best at.

Lindsey Rose was sent to prison for life with no possibility of parole on 3 September 1998, for the shooting murders of Edward Cavanagh and Cavanagh's girlfriend Carmelita Lee in 1984, the stabbing murder of Reynette Holford in 1987 and the shooting and stabbing murders of two Sydney prostitutes, Kerrie Pang and Fatima Ozonal, in February 1994.

Little is known of Rose before his career as a killer, except that he was one of the ambulance officers at the scene of the horrific Granville train disaster in Sydney's

Lindsey Robert Rose

inner west on 18 January 1977 – 83 people were killed and another 220 injured when a peak-hour morning train was flattened under tonnes of concrete after it had struck a bridge pylon.

Rose was one of the many paramedic heroes who worked without sleep, tending to the trapped and injured and bringing the bodies out of the wreckage at considerable risk to their own lives.

At the time of his arrest in 1997, Rose was said to be working as a maintenance fitter, earning about $1500 per month.

Rose's first victim was Edward 'Billy' Cavanagh, a 58-year-old standover man and associate of the late crime boss Robert 'Aussie Bob' Trimbole. Apparently Cavanagh had bashed a friend of Rose's, David Norton, and, armed with a shortened .22 rifle, Rose and an accomplice went to Cavanagh's Hoxton Park home on the night of 21 January 1984, seeking retribution.

Cavanagh was out when they arrived, so Rose and his accomplice bound Cavanagh's 21-year-old Filipina de facto wife, Carmelita Lee, who was naked and about to have a bath, to a bed with a telephone cord, and waited for Cavanagh to come home.

When Cavanagh walked through the door cradling two dozen oysters he had brought at the local pub, Rose opened fire. In his confession to police he described the killing: 'He hit the deck and fell ... then I shot, shot, shot, shot.'

Rose and the accomplice, who has since been charged with the two murders, then dragged Cavanagh into the bedroom and 'shot him a further few times' before shooting Carmelita Lee four times in the head

The St Valentine's Day Murderer

at close range. Rose told police: 'I had to kill her. She was there.' Police found eight spent cartridges at the scene of the murders.

In 1987, while burgling the West Ryde home of wealthy property developer, 78-year-old Bill Graf, who was sleeping in a bedroom nearby, Rose was interrupted by Graf's de facto wife of 20 years, Reynette Holford, who leapt at him with a pair of scissors.

In his confession to this crime, after he was arrested in 1997, Rose told police that when Reynette Holford found him in the house 'she had a pair of scissors in her hand and lunged at me with the scissors, which shocked the hell out of me'.

Rose said he 'thumped her a couple of times to stop her screaming' in the struggle that followed, then killed her by stabbing her about the neck and face 32 times with a screwdriver and strangling her. Rose told police later that her death was a 'mistake'.

Before Lindsey Rose confessed to the murder of Reynette Holford, Bill Graf had been suspected by police of committing the murder. He died in 1987 without the real culprit having been charged, without knowing that his name would be cleared.

Rose's next murder was a 'contract killing' and once again, as in the murder of Carmelita Lee, an innocent victim would be in the wrong place at the wrong time and be murdered to protect Rose's identity.

At 7.30 pm on St Valentine's Day 1994, Rose and an accomplice, unemployed tattoo artist Ronald Lewis Waters, 33, went to a Gladesville massage parlour, 'Kerrie's Oasis Reflexology and Relaxation Clinic'.

But it was murder, not sex, that they had on their minds.

Lindsey Robert Rose

Rose had allegedly been offered $20,000 to kill the parlour's owner – Kerrie Pang, a 36-year-old divorced mother of five children (ranging from 15 months to 15 years) – by her de facto husband, but when he and Waters arrived at the parlour, they were greeted by employee Fatima Ozonal instead.

Fatima Ozonal, 25, a divorced mother of a 6-year-old girl, was forced at gunpoint to sit in the lounge of the parlour and wait for Kerrie Pang to arrive at work. While they waited, Rose shot Fatima Ozonal four times in the head at point blank range.

When Kerrie Pang arrived, Rose chased her along the hall, stabbed her 18 times in the face, chest and head and slit her throat before shooting her in the eye and setting the parlour alight.

Rose eventually came unstuck when his friend and confidant, a disgraced detective, revealed in a six-hour session before the NSW Crime Commission that he knew of the killings and that he had supplied Rose with the revolver that was believed to have been used in two of the shootings.

With the police hot on his tail, Rose fled Sydney in July 1996 and became the subject of a huge manhunt. At one stage he was listed as Australia's most wanted man. He was eventually located in Adelaide and arrested without incident at the suburb of Glenelg by SA detectives. He was extradited to Sydney in April 1997.

When he was charged with the murders of the two women in the massage parlour, Rose confessed to the Cavanagh, Lee and Holford murders as well.

His alleged accomplice in the St Valentine's Day murders, Ronald Waters, admitted to being at the

The St Valentine's Day Murderer

massage parlour on the night in question and named Rose as the killer. Waters was committed for trial for Kerrie Pang's murder but the charge of murdering Fatima Ozonal was dismissed.

Lindsey Robert Rose, the St Valentine's Day Murderer, and killer of three other people, is in jail for the rest of his life, never to be released.

Chapter 24

ARTHUR STANLEY 'NEDDY' SMITH

Australia's Most Notorious Gangster

The face of the 48-year-old man sitting in the witness box could have been carved out of granite. It was expressionless as he gave evidence in a voice that seemed to show total disregard for discipline or reprimand. It was a face hardened by a life in the streets and prison. It was the face of Neddy Smith – underworld enforcer, gunman, rapist, heroin dealer, armed robber, murderer and Crown informer.

Neddy was dobbing in the cops.

Council assisting the 1993 Independent Commission Against Corruption (ICAC), Barry Toomey QC, was nursing his most prized stool pigeon through the evidence that, if proven, could bring the NSW Police Force to its knees.

Neddy was already the most notorious criminal in the country. Now he looked like becoming the most important informer in the nation's history. Although intellectually in command, Neddy was unable to control the continual shaking down the right side of his body and his right arm, the only noticeable signs of the advanced stages of Parkinson's disease, which had been affecting him for a decade.

In true gangland tradition, Neddy had refused to inform on any of his underworld mates. But he didn't bat an eyelid as he shelved the cops he had allegedly done business with over the years – the business of murder, bribery, drug trafficking, armed robbery and extortion. There seemed to have been corruption at every level. According to Neddy, the cops ran the lot. But Neddy had absolutely nothing to lose. After all, he was already doing life for murder and an additional 13 years for attempted armed robbery.

Neddy had had enough of life behind bars and didn't want to die there. The only way out was to rat on his alleged former business associates in the hope that the authorities would show him some leniency so he could die in his own bed with his family around him.

Under the deal he had done with the ICAC, Neddy was immune from prosecution for any previous offence (except murder) that he admitted being party to. With normal remissions on his current sentence, the best possible result he could expect was 6 years. But with Neddy's track record, that seemed highly unlikely. Horses had won Melbourne Cups with less form than Neddy. So Neddy went against his own rules and turned 'dog'.

Neddy's rat cunning and ability to negotiate between all the warring factions of the Sydney underworld had seen his seemingly invincible rise to the top of his profession, without having a criminal conviction recorded in nearly a decade.

But times had changed, and here he was, back in a

Arthur Stanley 'Neddy' Smith

jail cell. He must have spent a lot of long lonely hours in his cell wondering how the hell he had wound up back in the joint.

Everything had been running like clockwork. He had created fear and havoc wherever he went. Neddy was the man. A real tough guy. But, as his associates put it, Neddy had fucked up something terrible.

Arthur Stanley 'Neddy' Smith was born in the inner Sydney working-class suburb of Redfern on 27 November 1944. He was the second of six children in a fatherless family. By the time he was 14, Neddy had had enough of Cleveland Street Boys' High School and had decided on a life of crime.

Between 1959 and 1961 young Neddy was in and out of institutions for stealing, assault, and breaking and entering. In May 1963, Neddy was sentenced to 6 years in jail on 13 counts of breaking, entering and stealing.

Those prison years taught Neddy to be as tough as nails. He emerged from jail early in 1967 over 180 cm tall, weighing 100 kg, and with a reputation as a man who was afraid of no one and who could fight like a threshing machine.

In June 1967, Neddy and Robert Arthur 'Bobby' Chapman were convicted of the violent rape of a 20-year-old Petersham housewife and sentenced to 12 years in prison with a minimum term of 7 years. When sentencing the two men, Justice Reynolds said that the woman had been raped in circumstances of 'appalling depravity'. The judge told Smith that his action of 'spitting on the woman when raping her indicated a warped and perverted mind'.

Neddy served his time in the toughest jails in

Australia's Most Notorious Gangster

NSW – Long Bay, Parramatta and Grafton. In March 1975, Neddy was released, tougher than ever. In November 1976, he was arrested by Detective Sergeant Roger Rogerson, then with the Armed Hold-Up Squad, and charged with two counts of shooting with intent to murder together with assault with attempt to rob, attempted armed robbery and possessing an unlicensed pistol.

But, as was to be the case in most of Neddy's future arrests, it was found that there was no case to answer on any of the charges except that of possessing an unlicensed pistol. Neddy's conviction on the pistol charge was later quashed on appeal.

A short time after this, Neddy became Rogerson's underworld informant.

By early 1977, Neddy's financial situation had improved dramatically and he bought a house in the inner western suburb of Sydenham. He turned it into an electronic fortress, surrounded by 3-metre walls, with security doors and windows and closed-circuit television surveillance cameras.

While those close to Neddy maintained that the almost paranoid level of security was to protect his family, police thought differently. They believed that it was to prevent Neddy being robbed of a valuable substance – heroin. Lots of it.

Their suspicions were confirmed in 1978 when Neddy's tapped telephone revealed startling information about a heroin-smuggling ring that was responsible for shifting up to 11.3 kg of the drug every month. This was one of the biggest operations in the country, and represented about 15% of the NSW heroin consumption in 1978.

Arthur Stanley 'Neddy' Smith

Justice Stewart's 1985 Royal Commission report into the heroin ring revealed how the gang had come unstuck: 'By listening to Smith's conversations it was learnt that Smith was organising and financing heroin importation from Thailand. The names of a Bangkok bar owner, William (Bill) Sinclair, a Manly hairdresser, Warren Fellows, and Paul Hayward, a well-known Newtown Rugby League football star, as well as others involved, were mentioned, and details of the importation were discussed.'

NSW police passed on the information to Thai authorities and Sinclair, Fellows and Hayward were arrested in Bangkok and charged with possession of 8.4 kg of the highest-quality No 4 Golden Dragon Pearl heroin, worth about $3 million retail on the streets of Sydney.

All three were convicted and given long jail sentences. Bill Sinclair vehemently maintained his innocence and on appeal was granted a new trial. On 24 January 1983, he was acquitted, and returned to Australia.

It was later revealed that the most active courier, 26-year-old Fellows, was paid $60,000 per trip to bring suitcases with as much as 13 kg of Thai heroin through Australian Customs.

On 12 October 1978, the day after the arrest of Sinclair, Fellows and Hayward in Bangkok, police raided Neddy's fortress in Sydenham and found $39,360 in cash and a receipt for a safety deposit box at the Marrickville branch of the ANZ bank. In the box they found $90,100 in cash, $10,000 worth of diamonds and a short manual on how to get a container past customs.

Neddy and his de facto wife, Debra Joy Smith, were charged with possession of money unlawfully obtained.

Australia's Most Notorious Gangster

In the following weeks, drug squad detectives raided homes all over Sydney, and recovered hundreds of thousands of dollars in cash and vast amounts of heroin. One of the villains arrested was Neddy's stepbrother, Edwin 'Teddy' Smith, who was found in possession of 1.5 kg of high-grade heroin. Teddy pleaded guilty and was sentenced to 10 years in the slammer.

Neddy was charged with having 'goods in custody' (the $39,360), for which he received 6 months. As he had also violated his parole, obviously, Neddy now looking at finishing off the 4 years outstanding from the 1967 rape sentencing.

Through a succession of appeals to the High Court by Neddy's battery of highly paid legal advisors, Neddy was released in October 1980, two years earlier than expected.

Out of the can, Neddy teamed up with Warren Lanfranchi, a heroin dealer and thief he had met in prison. By mid–1981, Lanfranchi was having problems with the cops. They desperately wanted to have a chat with him about several bank robberies and the attempted murder of a police officer – Lanfranchi had allegedly aimed a handgun at a traffic officer's face and pulled the trigger, but the gun misfired.

As Lanfranchi would find out soon enough, the police don't like people who try to kill their fellow officers.

The 22-year-old Lanfranchi didn't want to go back to prison, and had made it known that if cornered by police, he would shoot it out. But there was an easier way. Neddy allegedly offered his friend Detective Sergeant Roger Rogerson $50,000, on Lanfranchi's behalf, to have the investigations dropped. Rogerson agreed to discuss the matter and a meeting with Lanfranchi was arranged through the ever-obliging Neddy.

On the Saturday afternoon of 27 June 1981, Neddy drove Warren Lanfranchi, in a green BMW, to a narrow lane called Dangar Place, in Chippendale, just a few minutes' drive from the heart of Sydney. According to his girlfriend, Sallie Anne Huckstepp, Lanfranchi had $10,000 in $50 bills stuffed down the front of his trousers and was unarmed when he left home for the meeting.

At 2.50 pm, Neddy parked the BMW near the entrance to Dangar Place and watched as Warren Lanfranchi walked with his hands above his head down the lane toward Rogerson, about 40 metres away. What Lanfranchi didn't know was that Rogerson was not alone. The laneway was completely surrounded by 18 heavily armed police.

According to Rogerson's statement, Lanfranchi said to him as they finally met face to face: 'I can't do any more jail. Are we going to do business?' Rogerson replied: 'There is no business. We are here to arrest you for the attempted murder of a police officer.'

Realising that he had walked into a trap, Lanfranchi allegedly produced a gun from the front of his trousers and aimed it at Rogerson, who also drew a gun and shot Lanfranchi twice, in the neck and the heart, killing him instantly. Lanfranchi had not fired a shot.

The gun found lying beside Lanfranchi's body was over 20 years old and had a defective firing mechanism. The gun had no fingerprints on it. And there was no sign of the alleged $10,000 that Lanfranchi's girlfriend said he had had when he left home.

The November 1981 coronial inquiry into the shooting of Warren Lanfranchi found, thanks largely to evidence given by Neddy Smith, that Detective Sergeant Roger Caleb Rogerson had protected himself 'while endeavouring to effect an arrest'.

Acting for the Lanfranchi family, Ian Barker QC said that it was open to conjecture as to 'whether the deceased did in fact have a gun at the material time'.

As Smith would later testify in court, it was soon after he had delivered Lanfranchi that crooked police decided to give him the keys to the city of Sydney, referred to as the 'Green Light' – Neddy now had permission to carry out armed hold-ups, bash anyone who got in his way, run SP premises and sell narcotics without fear of apprehension.

Naturally, the crooked cops wanted their whack. The only condition attached to the Green Light was that Neddy wasn't allowed to kill or harm a police officer. Apart from that, it was open slather.

But while Neddy was endearing himself to the police by carrying out armed hold-ups – he was sometimes driven away from crime scenes in a police car – things weren't looking good on the heroin charge from a couple of years earlier.

His stepbrother Teddy had had enough of being in the nick and had cut a deal with the Federal Police. He would tell them everything he knew about Neddy's alleged heroin dealing in exchange for remissions on his jail term and immunity from further prosecution.

At the 1980 Woodward Royal Commission into drug trafficking in NSW, Teddy sang like a nightingale, and became the first hood in NSW ever to spill the beans on organised crime.

Arthur Stanley 'Neddy' Smith

Teddy Smith told the Commission that he had been inside Neddy's Sydenham fortress when he took delivery of a suitcase containing 30 one-pound bags of pure heroin. Teddy claimed that Neddy started dancing around the room saying: 'I'm rich! I'm rich!'

Teddy further claimed that by using an ordinary domestic blender to remove the lumps, Neddy adulterated 13 oz of pure No 4 Golden Dragon Pearl heroin with 3 oz of Glucodin powder to make up one-pound packets, which he sold in sealed plastic bags.

Packaging the 3 oz shares removed from each pound into 1 oz and 2 oz packets, he sold them to friendly dealers without the knowledge of his partners.

Teddy alleged to the Commission that during mid–1978 he made three deliveries a day for Neddy of half-pound and one-pound packets of heroin to cars parked in Sydney's eastern suburbs. Driving past the assigned car at slow speed, he would drop the package into the vehicle's back window, which was wound down a few centimetres. At the peak of the operation, Neddy employed 14 people and was moving up to 25 pounds of heroin a month.

And Neddy was rich. Very rich. His stable of cars included a BMW, a Mercedes and a Porsche. Neddy owned the fortress at Sydenham, a half share in a $17,000 speedboat and a large amount of jewellery, including a $32,000 diamond ring.

According to Teddy Smith, Neddy had once told him that while there were millionaires in the world who had it in assets, 'he would be one of the only ones who had it in cash'.

On the strength of his stepbrother's evidence, Neddy was charged with conspiracy to supply heroin.

Australia's Most Notorious Gangster

On the second day of Neddy's trial in May 1980, the prime witness, Teddy, had a sudden change of heart and admitted to the court that he had deliberately given false evidence and that everything he had said about Neddy's involvement in the heroin trade was fabricated. Neddy was really a choirboy who was misunderstood. The prosecution lawyers were, understandably, furious.

Judge Alistair Muir instructed the jury that on the grounds of lack of evidence, Neddy must be acquitted.

But change of heart or not, the non-parole period of Edwin William Teddy Smith's 10-year sentence for heroin possession was reduced considerably – it would now run from his arrest on 27 October 1978 to 26 August 1982. When eventually released from prison, Teddy Smith left town in a hurry.

During the next seven years, thanks to the Green Light, Neddy continued to lead a charmed life, and he became the highest-profile gangster in the history of organised crime in this country.

In the '80s, under the protection of the Green Light, Smith and his gang netted over $600,000 from armed robberies, operated one of the biggest SP betting networks in Australia and made a fortune by importing and distributing millions of dollars' worth of drugs.

It was the era of the infamous NSW Gang Wars, when opposed underworld factions fought it out, sometimes in the streets, for control of the lucrative drug trade. It seemed that someone was getting shot almost every day. Neddy usually managed to get a mention in the press somewhere, but emerged from it all unscathed.

Arthur Stanley 'Neddy' Smith

And his luck held again on the morning of 2 April 1986. As he left the Iron Duke Hotel in the inner-Sydney working-class suburb of Waterloo and was walking to his car, a Holden sedan burst from behind a line of trees, mounted the footpath and ran into Neddy, slamming him against a wall. He was lucky not to have been killed.

The badly-battered gangster managed to drag himself back to the hotel to wait for an ambulance. Diagnosed as having six broken ribs, a broken leg and suspected fractures of the spine, a heavily plastered and bandaged Neddy was interviewed and photographed by TV news crews and the press the following day as he was eased into a car in front of the hospital after defying the doctors' orders and discharging himself.

The next day, on crutches, Neddy arrived at Channel 9 by helicopter and appeared on *Willesee*, where he described himself as an 'average knockabout bloke' whose reputation as an underworld figure and enforcer was a fabrication of the media and was totally undeserved.

Neddy told interviewer Ray Martin that he knew the driver of the car which ran him over. 'This man is in close with the police,' he said. 'The police and certain crooks want me out of the way so they have teamed up. I have trodden on quite a few toes.'

Neddy said that he was an invalid pensioner who had suffered from Parkinson's disease for six years and used the pension, gambling, borrowing from friends and sometimes stealing to provide for his wife and family.

He admitted that at one stage he had been a 'debt collector and standover man', but claimed he had never had to 'thump anyone'. He maintained that he was broke and 'didn't have two bob to rub together'.

Australia's Most Notorious Gangster

On 26 April 1986, 41-year-old Sydney pensioner Terrence Edwin Ball was charged with the attempted hit-and-run murder of Neddy Smith. At Ball's trial, Neddy failed to identify him as the man who tried to run him over, and the charge was dismissed.

After more press than even the high-profile Neddy could take, he decided to move his wife Debra and their three young children to the NSW city of Newcastle, about 160 km north of Sydney.

The Smiths' transport – a Rolls Royce or a Mercedes Benz – would change every couple of months, and it became routine that a car would pick Neddy up on the Monday morning and return him on the Friday night to spend the weekend around the pool with Debra and the kids.

On 30 October 1987, Neddy Smith did something very uncharacteristic. In a drunken frenzy, he committed murder in a very public place and in front of about 70 witnesses.

It should never have happened. Over a minor traffic altercation, Neddy stabbed another motorist to death in busy Coogee Bay Road. Only hours later he was picked up and charged with murder.

Amid howls of protest from the State Opposition, on 2 December 1987, Neddy was granted bail of $50,000 on the murder charge; bail had been formally refused twice at earlier hearings. Bail was granted on the grounds that Neddy hadn't had a conviction in eight years, was the father of three children and was in the advanced stages of Parkinson's disease.

On 21 December 1988, police spotted Neddy and a couple of men 'casing' the Botany Council Chambers in South Sydney. The fact that the $160,000 Christmas

Arthur Stanley 'Neddy' Smith

payroll was due to arrive the next morning was probably no coincidence.

At dawn the following day, armed police took up positions in the Council building, the nearby fire station and other locations. After the payroll vans arrived, Armed Hold-Up Squad detectives approached a white Holden panel van parked nearby and told its occupants to come out with their hands in the air.

Neddy Smith, Glen Roderick Flack, 32, and Richard John Harris, 27, emerged from the van wearing green sloppy joes and white gloves. A search of the van revealed a loaded .357 magnum pistol, a sawn-off 12-gauge shotgun, two black balaclavas, a walkie-talkie and a carry bag.

There was no bail for Neddy this time. At his trial, on 9 September 1989, he pleaded guilty to all charges relating to the bungled robbery attempt, and was given 13 years. But that was only the half of it. He still had his murder trial to come.

At that trial on 20 February 1990, the court was told by Mark Tedeschi QC, for the Crown, that on the day of the alleged murder, Neddy had spent most of the day drinking with a friend. He was on his way along Coogee Bay Road to the Coogee Sports Club at about 9.00 pm that night.

'For some unknown reason, the Honda, which was owned by Smith's wife but driven by his friend, stopped in the line of traffic. A tow truck behind them could not pass and its driver, Mr Thomas Millane, flashed his lights a couple of times,' Tedeschi told the court.

The Crown alleged that Smith and his companion got out of their car and began fighting with Millane and his passenger, 34-year-old Ronnie Flavell. Millane heard Flavell call for help before seeing his friend lying on his back over the bonnet of a car parked nearby, the jury heard.

Smith was standing over Flavell and Millane saw what he thought was Smith punching Flavell with his free hand. But as he pulled Smith away, Millane noticed a bloodied knife in Smith's hand. The jury heard that Smith threatened Millane with the knife before jumping back into his car and driving away. Ronnie Flavell died shortly after, on the operating table in the Prince of Wales Hospital at Randwick.

Neddy was found guilty of murder, and on 16 March 1990, Justice McInerney sentenced him to life imprisonment. But as the killing took place in 1987, before the 1989 truth-in-sentencing legislation, the sentence could be reduced to a fixed term on appeal, and Neddy could hold out expectations of someday being released.

In order to give himself some sort of a chance at ever getting out of jail to die in his own bed, Neddy started talking to the ICAC in mid–1992.

But even a life sentence for murder and 13 years for armed robbery couldn't keep Neddy Smith out of the headlines. Neddy was immortalised in the 1996 award-winning ABC TV program, *Blue Murder*, about the life and times of Roger Rogerson and Neddy and all the old gang of everyone's favourite cops, killers and cut-throats. The program has never been shown in NSW because of Neddy's seemingly endless appearances in court on murder charges.

In 1995, he was charged with seven murders from the 'good old days'. At his committal hearing in September 1996, after charges of murdering drug

Arthur Stanley 'Neddy' Smith

dealers Barry Croft, Barry McCann, Danny Chubb and Bruce Sandery were dropped, the charges were reduced to three: the murders of Warren Lanfranchi's girlfriend, Sallie Anne Huckstepp, drug dealer Lewton Shu and Smith's drinking mate, brothel-keeper, drug dealer and debt collector, the gun totin' Harvey Francois Jones.

Jones, 29, fancied himself as a gangster and was notorious for producing giant hand guns in bars and other public houses and shooting the places up while in Neddy's company. It was common knowledge that Jones had become an embarrassment and that Neddy was becoming increasingly tired of the troublesome gunslinger who wouldn't go away.

At Neddy's trial for the murder of Harvey Jones, which lasted eight weeks and ended on 9 September 1998, the Crown alleged that Jones was picked up from the Star Hotel in Alexandria on 15 July 1983 by Neddy, who drove him to Botany Bay, shot him dead and ordered his driver to bury the body. The body was discovered in March 1995, by a man looking for coins washed up by the tide.

It was believed that Jones had been carrying up to $60,000 in cash at the time of his murder. The money was to bribe police through Smith, to get him off charges of shooting up a tavern.

In 1994, while he was doing time for the murder of Ronnie Flavell, Neddy made the fatal mistake of telling his cell mate, who had been wired by the police, that he (Smith) had murdered Jones and buried his body on the foreshore of Botany Bay.

The hushed court listened to the tape of Smith telling of the killing of his friend: 'When I got him he said, "I'd die for you". I said, "You're about to, ya fuckin' mug" ... Blew his heart out with a big three five seven.'

And if the tapes weren't enough to send Neddy back to jail for a second life term, this time under the truth-in-sentencing legislation, Neddy's driver, code-named Mr Green, gave evidence that he witnessed the killing and buried the body in the Botany Bay sandhills at Smith's behest.

It took the jury six days to find Neddy guilty of murdering Harvey Jones. In sentencing Neddy Smith to life imprisonment without the possibility of parole, Justice Carolyn Simpson suggested that the term was academic.

Justice Simpson said that 53-year-old Smith has suffered from Parkinson's disease for 18 years and even a lesser term could have outlasted his lifespan. Justice Simpson added that the 1983 murder of Jones was 'cold-blooded, premeditated, and deliberate' and that Smith had shown no remorse.

'The killing was committed for at least three reasons,' Justice Simpson said. 'One, for monetary gain; two, to protect and preserve the prisoner's own criminal empire; and three, because Jones had become a nuisance and a pest to the prisoner.'

Justice Simpson concluded: 'The prisoner's criminal record, as I have stated it, alone disentitles the prisoner to any claim for leniency. Arthur Stanley Smith, you are sentenced to penal servitude for life.'

And at the time of writing (September 1998) Neddy still has the murder trials of Huckstepp and Shu to come. But it is debatable whether the ageing gangster will live long enough to face another trial.

Arthur Stanley 'Neddy' Smith

Neddy Smith has countless enemies, the main one being time itself. His Parkinson's disease is now so bad that Smith was barely audible at times while giving evidence during the Jones trial, and his head would roll about uncontrollably.

One of his associates who has observed the progress of Neddy's Parkinson's disease (which Neddy calls 'me shakes') over the years told a *Sydney Morning Herald* reporter: 'He shakes like a dog shitting razor blades. He'll never live it out.'

And there would be no shortage of people who would hope that this is true. For a million different reasons.

But one thing is for certain – Australia's most notorious gangster of the '80s and '90s will die behind bars for his crimes. Neddy Smith is 'never to be released'.

www.ingramcontent.com/pod-product-compliance
Lightning Source LLC
Chambersburg PA
CBHW022050290426
44109CB00014B/1047